IMAGES
of America

FORT CLARK AND BRACKETTVILLE
LAND OF HEROES

IMAGES
of America

FORT CLARK AND BRACKETTVILLE
LAND OF HEROES

William F. Haenn

ARCADIA
PUBLISHING

Published by Arcadia Publishing
Charleston, South Carolina

Library of Congress Catalog Card Number: 2002105248

For all general information contact Arcadia Publishing at:
Telephone 843-853-2070
Fax 843-853-0044
E-Mail sales@arcadiapublishing.com
For customer service and orders:
Toll-Free 1-888-313-2665

Visit us on the Internet at www.arcadiapublishing.com

SEMINOLE-NEGRO INDIAN SCOUT DETACHMENT 1ST SERGEANT BEN JULY, C. 1896. This photograph of Sergeant July, standing at parade-rest armed with his Springfield carbine, was taken in the Seminole Camp on the Fort Clark Military Reservation. The Scouts were then operating out of Fort Duncan at Eagle Pass, but returned frequently to "the camp" to visit their families. In all likelihood, also pictured are Sergeant July's children and his home. (Robert J. Sporleder Album, Fort Clark Historical Society)

CONTENTS

ACKNOWLEDGMENTS

Familiar, everything was remarkably familiar! That was the overpowering feeling I got when I crossed Las Moras creek for the first time and entered Fort Clark. I don't mean *deja vu*, I mean the familiar orderliness a soldier expects of a frontier military post with a row of barracks and a line of officer's quarters separated by a parade ground, a guardhouse, mess halls, hospital, headquarters building, stables, and commissary. It was all still there, in limestone no less! But there were more 20th century facilities, including a theater, an officer's club, and an enormous swimming pool—all this and magnificent trees. How could I have not heard of this place? A feature article about Fort Clark in *Texas Highways Magazine* brought me here in 1987. I never intend to leave.

My lifelong passion for history was nurtured in my youth by my mother on visits to Independence Hall, Valley Forge, and Gettysburg. She bought me my first book, *Robert E. Lee and the Road to Honor*, and that did it. While in college I met a compelling character by the name of George E. Gorman, who made a living buying and selling militaria. George, more than any other person, influenced me to become a soldier. It was a perfect fit and came easily to me, being a soldier. So there you have it, a soldier who loves history and along came Fort Clark and the opportunity to live where soldiers made history. Who could ask for more?

At first Fort Clark's history was a bit confusing, particularly the lingering fantasy history promoted by the civilian owners of the fort. However, I was fortunate to have neighbors who had immersed themselves in the history of Fort Clark and they mentored me. Don Swanson, Ben Pingenot, and Charles Downing were the first heroes I met here and those gentlemen shared with me their knowledge and enthusiasm for Fort Clark. Many of the photographs used to tell Fort Clark's story were gathered by Charlie and Ben over their lifetimes. Their treasured images have passed into other hands now to be viewed by new generations.

I am fascinated by the photograph's ability to catch a little of the spirit of its subject, just as Native Americans suspected. I have tried to convey that spirit here by telling a story of the hero that resides in each one of us and how a place in time can bring forth that hero. I hope I succeeded and both the reader and the generous providers of the photographs judge this work to have merit.

The single most critical element in this undertaking was the photographs! It was my exceptional good fortune to be trusted with these treasures and even more importantly to know these heroes as my friends: first and foremost the Fort Clark Historical Society, who gave me access to their archives; Zack Davis, who shared his premier collection of Brackettville views; Chris Hale, who rescued Ben Pingenot's collection and brought it home; Virginia Shahan, Happy's wife, and Tulisha Wardlaw, his daughter, who have smiles as big as Texas; Genell Hobbs, who can find anything; James W. Zintgraff, who has the magic; Mary Helen Kreiger, a local girl who married a soldier and still has a twinkle in her eye; Lyn Vinton Beliveau, Lt. French's granddaughter and transcriber of his diaries, who has enriched my life; Aida Nettleton, who drew the maps and always makes the journey to Seminole Canyon worth the effort; Rosantina Calvetti at Warren Studios in Del Rio who found some jewels; Alisa Mauldin at the U.S. Military Academy Archives who came through; Anne Gallon at Dale Gallon Galleries who had a key ingredient; and William and Ethel Warrior, who embody the character and genuine humanity of the Seminole people.

Encouragement fuels accomplishment and there are several people who, unknowingly perhaps, helped me to endeavor to persevere: Pat and Fran Owens, with whom I share Quarters

No. 25–26 and who years ago challenged me to write a book about Fort Clark; Steve and Judy Crosby whose enthusiasm was infectious; Flo Dean from the *Brackett News* who always wanted to know how the book was coming along; Betty Winters who kept my spirits up with email and phone calls; my mother who made sure I didn't starve, and my brother Michael who made sure my house didn't fall apart; fellow Arcadia author Doug Braudaway who said I could do it and to make the reader care about each photo; and the ladies who put up with me throughout, Gene Slate and Elizabeth Luna.

Soldiers have always been my heroes and this book is about heroes. My personal hero is a soldier and to her this effort is dedicated: my daughter, Margaret Haenn Vineyard (USMA 99), Captain U.S. Army Signal Corps.

2002 is the Sesquicentennial of the establishment of Fort Clark and I hope this book in some small way helps recognize and celebrate that historic milestone. Should the reader ever visit Fort Clark and Brackettville, it is the intent of this book to make that experience more familiar. Vaya con Dios.

INTRODUCTION

If geography is the stage, then history is the play! For the history of Fort Clark and Brackettville center stage was a tranquil pond of cool water sheltered in a grove of ancient twisted live oak trees. The source was Las Moras Spring, named by the Spanish conquistadors for the mulberry trees lining the banks of the creek that flowed from it to the Rio Grande. An ancient camping ground visited by man for millennia before the Spanish came, the site has seen continuous use for perhaps the past 12,000 years. A chain of national events in 1848 forever changed the area and gave it a rendezvous with destiny. The discovery of gold in California and the Treaty of Guadalupe Hidalgo precipitated the opening of the Lower Road from San Antonio to El Paso. Las Moras Spring sat adjacent to the road, and became a welcome resting place for travelers. To protect travelers on the road and to secure the spring, the U.S. Government established a fort on the high ground above the spring, south of the road. The establishment of the fort effectively closed the eastern branch of the Great Comanche War Trail, which had carried Indians to the spring for hundreds of years. To supply the fort and the travelers on the road, Oscar Brackett founded a town on the low ground to the north of the road, once again proving that, "commerce, not the invader, after all is the conqueror." The fort and its soldiers by necessity became the lifeblood of Brackettville, so a marriage of convenience took place, the town and the fort each needing the other to exist. In the antebellum heyday of stagecoaches traversing the "lower road" west to California, it took 24 torturous hours of bone jarring ride across a hog wallow prairie from San Antonio, before the coaches made Fort Clark their first overnight stop. In the 1850s Fort Clark's junior officers, who would advance to glory on the battlefields of Pennsylvania and Virginia, learned valuable lessons in soldiering, chasing elusive Comanches across Texas. All but abandoned during the Civil War, by the early 1870s Fort Clark had grown to become the largest military installation in Texas. National attention focused on Fort Clark in the spring of 1873 when President Grant ordered Colonel Mackenzie and the 4th Cavalry to ride into Mexico in pursuit of hostile Indians. In the vanguard of the raiders was a new and unique unit, the Seminole-Negro Indian Scout Detachment and its daring officer, Lt. John L. Bullis, both destined to become legendary in the annals of Texas military history. The Indians were gone by the time the railroad and the 19th Infantry came in 1882. One of this regiment's young lieutenants began a diary when he arrived, which illuminates daily life during the Victorian era of the garrison. The new century supplied several more generations of American youth who came to soldier in Texas. The post survived multiple attempts to close it over the years, all but the last. After 94 years of active service the fort quietly passed into history and the town faced the future alone. In those generations, to this place, came an honor roll of American heroes. Recognizable heroes like J.E.B. Stuart, James Longstreet, John Bell Hood, Fitzhugh Lee, George B. McClellan, Phillip H. Sheridan, William Tecumseh Sherman, Ranald S. Mackenzie, "Pecos Bill" Shafter, Abner Doubleday, George C. Marshall, George S. Patton Jr., and Jonathan M. Wainwright. Obscure heroes like Seminole Scouts Pompey Factor, Adam Paine, Isaac Payne, and John Ward, all recipients of the Congressional Medal of Honor, are buried here. Unsung heroes, the likes of the buffalo soldiers of every historic black regiment in the Army, the troopers of the Army's most celebrated cavalry regiments and its only black cavalry division, and the citizen soldiers of the Texas National Guard. They came to Fort Clark and Brackettville not intending to be heroes, just to serve their country, but history made them heroes. Following in their footsteps came new heroes to make movies about heroes, beginning with John Wayne and his epic film *The Alamo* in 1959. All their valiant spirits are still here, captured for the ages by the camera's eye. The majority of the photos that tell their story have never been published. They are true photographic treasures; images that were rescued by local collectors or more likely appeared unexpectedly from private sources and went safely into the Fort Clark Historical Society collection, never before seen photographs of Fort Clark's soldiers, buildings, and events. Surviving troopers, who served at Fort Clark, or their descendants, sent them to the Historical Society, somehow feeling Fort Clark is the place the picture should be. The leather bound and gold embossed *Robert J. Sporleder Album*, containing 33 1896 vintage photographs, was just such an incident of exceptional good fortune. Our genuine blessing is that heroes still come to this place and because of them Fort Clark survived and is unsurpassed as one of America's most complete frontier forts, with over 80 historic buildings, many still in use for their original intended purpose, comprising the largest National Register Historic District in private ownership west of the Mississippi. As long as there are heroes, Fort Clark and Brackettville will never be abandoned!

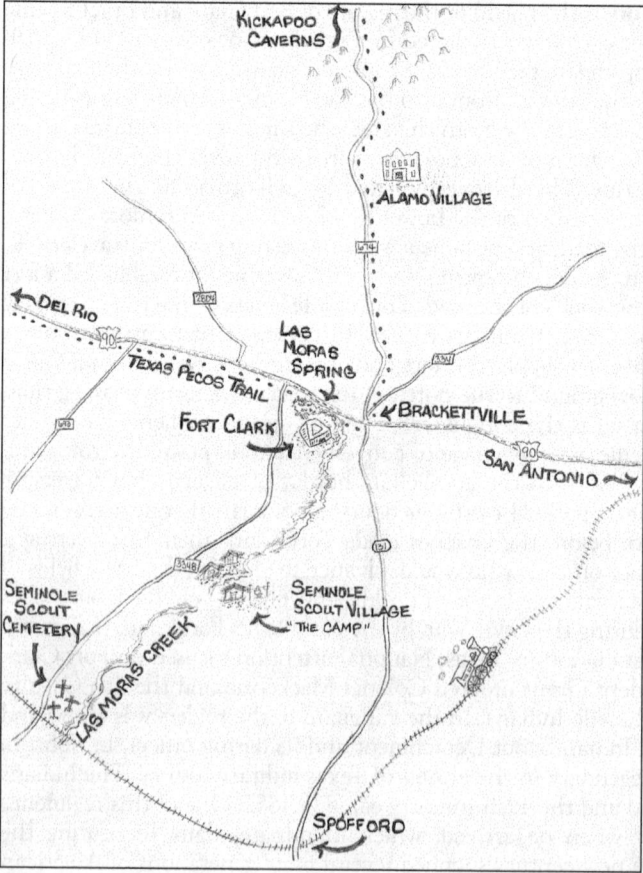

LAND OF HEROES. The spring, the fort, and the town of Brackettville sit astride the north-south axis of the eastern branch of the Great Comanche War Trail and the east-west axis of the Lower Road to California. (Drawn by Aida Nettleton)

One

LAS MORAS
THE SPRING AND ITS ROLE SINCE
ARCHAIC TIME

LAS MORAS SPRING AND THE POST SWIMMING POOL. Still surrounded by stands of ancient Spanish oaks and pecan trees, the spring's daily issue of six million gallons flows southeast into the pool and the spillway to form Las Moras creek, which empties into the Rio Grande some 30 miles away. The limestone shelf of high ground above the spring (top of picture) proved an ideal site for a fort, whose garrison would protect travelers on the road and secure the spring. At the bottom of the photo is the Municipal Utility District pump house. (Fort Clark Springs Association)

9

SPRING POND, C. 1896. To this quiet pool of cool water in archaic times came predator and prey, mammoth, bison, camel, horse, and the ancient Texan hunter-gatherers of the Lower Pecos region. Comanches habitually camped here on their annual trek into Mexico. In the late summer of 1590 the party of Spanish explorer Gaspar Castano de Sosa may have been the first Europeans to see the spring. An encounter between Conquistador Alonso de Leon's expedition and a lone survivor of LaSalle's failed expedition living among the Indians is thought to have occurred at the spring in 1688. "Las Moras" is first mentioned by the Spanish in 1767, naming the place for the mulberry trees lining the banks of the creek. (Robert J. Sporleder Album, Fort Clark Historical Society)

"THE GROVE" AT THE SPRING, C. 1896. The oak trees on all sides of the spring were not only a reliable indicator of the presence of abundant water but a welcome relief from the seemingly endless barren prairie. A resting place for millennia, countless generations of Native American peoples, early Spanish explorers, emigrants moving west, and soldiers protecting the frontier experienced the remarkable serenity of this site. Today these same trees shade and protect the Rendezvous Park picnic grove. (Robert J. Sporleder Album, Fort Clark Historical Society)

OAKS AND THE SPRING FROM THE WEST, C. 1896. A soldier stands among the oaks near a boy on a burro and two men on horseback on the west side of the spring. The spring pond is just beyond the trees in the open space. The tent to the left may also be seen in the top picture on the opposite page. It is always a popular and inviting place for picnics, walks in the shade, or the photographer's camera, where most memories of Fort Clark begin. (Robert J. Sporleder Album, Fort Clark Historical Society)

FILLING A WATER BARREL IN THE SPRING, C. 1880s. A boy watches as a civilian employee of the Quartermaster Corps fills a water barrel from the spring. On a daily basis an endless number of water barrels were filled by driving a cart into the spring and then hauling the barrels up the hill to the post for delivery to each barracks, mess hall, guardhouse, hospital, and officers' quarters. The regimental quartermaster, under the scrutiny of the post surgeon, was normally responsible for keeping fresh water in good supply. (William Hilderbrand, Gainesville, Texas, from glass negative)

SOLDIERS OF THE 3RD TEXAS INFANTRY AT THE SPRING IN 1898. The spring is now surrounded by a picket fence to keep out animals and to ensure the water is for "government" use only. The spring pond is clogged with water lilies, a persistent problem on the creek even today. The heavy iron pipe, which carried water to the post, is visible in the lower left-hand corner of the picture. The soldiers may just be posing for the photographer or actually working since there is a Quartermaster Sergeant and two armed privates on the plank pier, which reaches out into the pond to the spring opening. Brackettville is just on the other side of the fence. (Collection of Chris A. Hale)

PUMP HOUSE AT SPRING, C. 1890S. In 1895 a square wooden water tower was erected behind the line of company grade officers' quarters and water lines were installed to post buildings for the first time. A pump house was built at the spring to deliver water to the new water tower. The days of the water barrels were numbered as the technology of indoor plumbing greeted the new century. In this view the post is up the hill to the left front of the pump house and the plank pier is plainly visible on the right of the photograph. (Collection of Chris A. Hale)

SPRING POND CONTAINMENT WALL UNDER CONSTRUCTION, C. 1900. By the turn of the century a way to better control the spring began to take shape. Army engineers built a containment wall around the spring pond elevating the water at the southeast end, in the foreground of the picture, resulting in a stronger gravity flow of water out of the pond and into the creek, to the right of the picture. This not only helped solve the lily pad problem but also allowed for the creation of a swimming pool just below the spring. (Library of Congress)

SPRING POND AND POOL, C. 1920S. Although bathing and the washing of clothes in Las Moras creek is cited by post surgeons in their official reports as early as 1870, there is no recorded mention of swimming for recreation in 19th-century writings about life on the post. The first evidence of the existence of a swimming pool at the spring is the 1902 map of the Fort Clark Military Reservation. The pool, with its dirt bottom, retaining walls around the perimeter, raft, and sliding board, is in the foreground. The spring pond is in the upper right and the containment wall is visible in the center of the picture. (Photography Collection Harry Ransom Humanities Research Center, the University of Texas at Austin)

PUMP HOUSE AT SPRING, C. 1920S. With the World War ended, a new pump house replaced the worn out 19th-century structure. The carved stone on the front of the building reads, "Water Power 1919." A second water tower, this one of steel, had been installed next to the 1895 wooden tower earlier in the century. Now the post truly had a modern water system. Despite modernization efforts, the spring still required continuous cleaning as noted in the October 1928 Inspector General's Report, "A heavy growth of vegetation exists in the Las Moras Spring basin. The basin also affords a breeding place for fish and turtles, many of which have grown to large size." (Fort Clark Historical Society)

FORT CLARK SWIMMING POOL, 1926. The swimming pool at Fort Clark was a refreshing diversion from the monotony of soldiering and unquestionably the largest on any post in the Army. Soldiers' children who return today recall many a summer afternoon spent in its cool waters. They also remember the post regulation that restricted the pool to "officers only" after 1600 hours (4 pm). When Col. George S. Patton Jr. arrived at Fort Clark on July 24, 1938, to take command of the 5th Cavalry, he sent a note to his wife Beatrice of his initial impressions of his new duty station, "... *All one can do here is to Ride-Read Write & Swim.*" (Fort Clark Historical Society)

THE NEW SWIMMING POOL, 1939. An all-concrete, boat-shaped pool 100 feet wide and 300 feet long replaced the dirt bottom pool, which served for nearly 40 years, in 1939. The Work Projects Administration accomplished construction of the pool. Water enters the pool from the spring and flows through the pool into Las Moras creek. This flow-through system keeps the pool filled with one million gallons of fresh spring water at a constant 68 degrees. The inlet from the spring is at the top center of the photo. The building in the left foreground is the officers' bathhouse (the enlisted bathhouse was several hundred yards down the creek). (Fort Clark Historical Society)

15

POST SWIMMING POOL 1939. Brigadier General Jonathan M. Wainwright was the post commander when the pool was completed. His decision to open the pool to all ranks caused such resentment among his officers that an inspector general complaint was filed against Wainwright accusing him of diverting funds from other W.P.A. projects on the post in order to complete the pool. Many believe Wainwright's reassignment to the Philippines, in the fall of 1940, was in some way connected with the I.G. investigation. (Fort Clark Historical Society)

POST SWIMMING POOL, SUNDAY, AUGUST 6TH, 1944. The soldiers are gone, but the pool, the oaks, and the spring remain. This U.S. Army Signal Corps photo captures the tranquility and stillness of a place that gave life and enjoyment to the post garrison for 92 years. As it had always been, new people would come to experience the unrelenting flow of the spring into the creek. (U.S. Army Signal Corps)

16

Two

THE LOWER ROAD
ESTABLISHMENT OF THE FORT AND
THE ANTEBELLUM PERIOD

POST HEADQUARTERS BUILDING, C. 1885. On June 30, 1857, U.S. Navy Lieutenant Edward F. Beale, in command of a column that included 25 pack camels from Camp Verde bound for California, encamped at Las Moras Spring. Lieutenant Beale was invited by the officers of the garrison to witness Retreat on the parade. He recorded in his journal that, "a fine stone building is nearing completion." So the soul of Fort Clark is first described. Originally built to serve as the Commanding Officer's quarters, the building became the post headquarters in 1873. Key decisions in the life of the fort were made in this building; every famous officer who ever served at Fort Clark knew this building intimately. Images of this building in its many evolutions appear throughout the book. (National Archives)

JOHN COFFEE "JACK" HAYS. A Texas Ranger of considerable renown, Hays camped at Las Moras Spring in 1848 on his expedition with Sam Maverick to find a route west to El Paso. He is credited with naming the Devil's River. (National Archives)

SAMUEL AUGUSTUS MAVERICK. Maverick was a Texas patriot, adventurer, and businessman. On July 30, 1852, the U.S. signed a 20-year lease with Maverick for the land where Fort Clark had been established just one month before. (From Rena Maverick Green, ed., Memoirs of Mary Maverick)

MAJOR GENERAL WILLIAM F. SMITH (USMA 1845). As a lieutenant, Smith was second-in-command to classmate William H.C. Whiting on the 1849 military expedition, which recommended that a fort be located on the high ground above Las Moras Spring. (Library of Congress)

GENERAL (CSA) JOSEPH E. JOHNSTON (USMA 1829). In June 1849 Johnston directed the march of the 3rd Infantry with 275 wagons and 2,500 animals to El Paso, establishing the "Lower Road." He inspected Fort Clark in November 1859 as the Lieutenant Colonel of the 1st Cavalry. (Library of Congress)

MAJOR GENERAL (CSA) JAMES EWELL BROWN STUART (USMA 1854). Lt. J.E.B. Stuart served at Fort Clark in the Regiment of Mounted Rifles, 1854. The cavalier of the Confederacy, he died May 12, 1864, of wounds received at the battle of Yellow Tavern, Virginia. (U.S. Military Academy Archives)

LIEUTENANT GENERAL (CSA) JAMES LONGSTREET ("OLD PETE") (USMA 1842). Captain Longstreet served at Fort Clark in 1854 while assigned to the 8th Infantry. Scapegoat for the Confederate defeat at Gettysburg, Grant's minister to Turkey, and commissioner of Pacific Railroads under McKinley and Roosevelt, he died in 1904. (Library of Congress)

GENERAL (CSA) JOHN BELL HOOD (USMA 1853). Lieutenant Hood served at Fort Clark in 1857 with the newly organized 2nd Cavalry. Hood distinguished himself in several engagements with Comanches while in Texas. Fort Hood, in Killeen, Texas, is named for this officer. (Library of Congress)

MAJOR GENERAL (CSA AND USA) FITZHUGH LEE (USMA 1856). This nephew of Robert E. Lee served at Fort Clark in 1858, along with Hood, as a Lieutenant in the 2nd Cavalry. On May 13, 1859, in a fight with Comanche Indians, he was shot through the lungs with an arrow. He distinguished himself in the Civil War, was governor of Virginia, and a Major General of Volunteers in the Spanish-American War. (U.S. Military Academy Archives)

19

BRIGADIER GENERAL JOHN T. SPRAGUE. As a brevet major, Sprague led a large military train to El Paso in the summer of 1850. Encamped at Las Moras Spring on July 7, 1850, Sprague had an encounter with the Seminole-Negroes, en route to Mexico, who would return in a generation to form the famed Scout Detachment. (U.S. Army Military History Institute)

MAJOR GENERALL GEORGE B. MCCLELLAN (USMA 1846). As a captain in the Corps of Engineers, McClellan visited Fort Clark in 1855. He rose to command the Army of the Potomac in the early campaigns of the Civil War and opposed Lincoln as the Democratic presidential candidate in 1864. He was governor of New Jersey and forever known to cavalrymen as the inventor of the "McClellan Saddle." (U.S. Military Academy Archives)

SARGENT HOTEL. This was the stop on El Paso Street in Brackettville for the stage line operating on the "lower road" between San Antonio and El Paso. While staying overnight at the hotel, a traveler described the experience of being in Brackettville in 1876: *"We visited the town after supper, and you may imagine our surprise to find ourselves in the liveliest burg in West Texas, where the night life could only be compared to the saloons and gambling places that existed the early days of the gold excitement of California and the Klondike."* (Photo by the author)

CONFEDERATE TROOPS ON THE LAS MORAS, MARCH 1861. This woodcut appeared in *Harper's Weekly* in June 1861 and was the first drawing of Confederate troops in Texas to be published in the Civil War. The soldiers pictured are a detachment of 18 Confederate troops, under the command of Capt. Tervanion T. Teel, then camped at a bend of Las Moras creek to the east of the garrison, poised to accept the surrender of the post from four companies of the 3rd U.S. Infantry commanded by Captain (later Major General) George Sykes (USMA 1842). But for the restraint and coolness of this West Point trained officer, the events connected with this drawing could have resulted in the first shots of the Civil War being fired at Fort Clark, three full weeks before Fort Sumter. In March of 1861 all Federal installations in Texas were being surrendered to Confederate authorities. Tension built in the days preceding the surrender of Fort Clark as the Federal troops systematically destroyed post buildings, government stores, and put several homes in Brackett to the torch. On the day of the surrender, Tuesday, March 19, 1861, it had been agreed between the two commanding officers that a cannon salute would be fired before lowering the National Colors, followed by the raising of the Texas flag. The salute was fired and the colors lowered, but as the Federal flag was recovered the Union soldiers cut the halliard and yanked it from the pulley, preventing the Confederates from raising their flag. Captain Teel immediately sent men up the pole to run the rope back through the pulley. As the Federal troops marched off in the direction of San Antonio they set fire to the barracks, further frustrating the Confederates. Captain Teel reported to his superiors that his detachment occupied the garrison and was in full possession of all the public property, and added, "*I cannot close this report without mentioning Capt. Sykes of the Federal Army. This gentleman did all in his power to have the fire extinguished, and saved the houses near the burning building, and it was only by his energy and prompt action, that many other buildings were saved. No other officer or Company aided in the least.*" (Collection of Chris A. Hale)

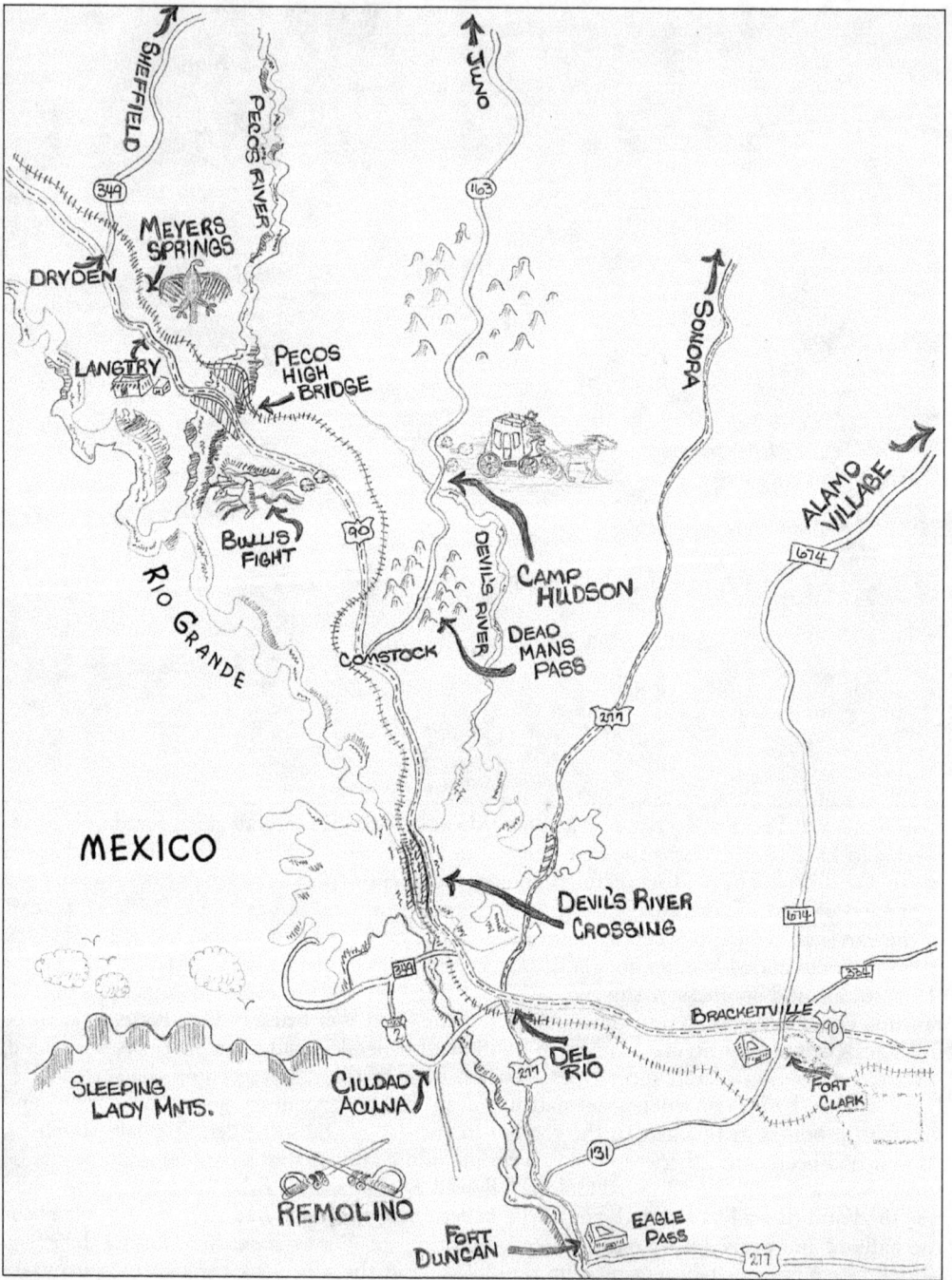

AREA OF OPERATIONS. (Drawn by Aida Nettleton, Comstock, Texas)

Three

FOOTSTEPS ECHO
POST CIVIL WAR TO
THE TURN OF THE CENTURY

POWDER MAGAZINE AND BRACKETTVILLE, C. 1887. This early view of the post east of the spring and just south of Las Moras creek was taken from the roof of the two-story cavalry barracks, which is now Bullis Hall. The small square building, where a group of soldiers and civilians have gathered for the photographer, is the powder magazine, one of the earliest post buildings, dating from 1854. The fenced building to the left is the first post guardhouse, then in use for storage (the Service Club now occupies the site). To the right of the magazine is the sutler's store compound (forerunner of the Post Exchange) operated by the post sutler, Mr. Friedlander, where soldiers could buy beer, play billiards, and socialize. The wagon bridge is visible just to the left and beyond the magazine. Oak trees line the creek and the town of Brackettville fills the horizon. The black corners on this image appear on several other images from the period and may indicate use of the same camera. (Collection of Chris A. Hale)

MAJOR GENERAL RANALD S. MACKENZIE (USMA 1862). Mackenzie served at Fort Clark as Colonel of the 41st Infantry 1868–69 and Post Commander as Colonel of the 4th Cavalry 1875. He led the raid to Remolino, Mexico on May 17, 1873. (U.S. Military Academy Archives)

MAJOR GENERAL WESLEY MERRITT (USMA 1860). Merritt was Post Commander as Lieutenant Colonel of the 9th Cavalry in 1873, U.S. Military Academy Superintendent in the 1880s, and Commander in Chief of the American Expeditionary Force to the Philippines in 1898. (U.S. Military Academy Archives)

MAJOR GENERAL WILLIAM R. "PECOS BILL" SHAFTER. Shafter was Post Commander as Lieutenant Colonel of the 24th Infantry 1869–78. A tireless campaigner, he was Commander in Chief of the American Expeditionary Force to Cuba in 1898, and received the Medal of Honor for gallantry in the Civil War. (National Archives)

GENERAL PHILIP H. SHERIDAN (USMA 1853). Sheridan visited Fort Clark with Secretary of War Belknap in March 1873 for secret meetings with Colonel Mackenzie, which precipitated the Remolino Raid. (U.S. Military Academy Archives)

24

GENERAL WILLIAM TECUMSEH SHERMAN
(USMA 1840). Sherman led an inspection
tour of Fort Clark in 1882 as Commander
in Chief of the United States Army. (U.S.
Military Academy Archives)

MAJOR GENERAL ZENUS R. BLISS (USMA
1854). He visited Fort Clark in 1854 enroute
to Fort Davis and returned in 1885 as
Lieutenant Colonel of the 19th Infantry. He
was awarded the Medal of Honor in 1898 for
gallantry in the Civil War. (U.S. Military
Academy Archives)

MAJOR GENERAL ABNER DOUBLEDAY
(USMA 1842). Doubleday served on court
martials duty at Fort Clark in 1871 as Colonel
of the 24th Infantry. Albert G. Spaulding
falsely credited him with inventing baseball.
(U.S. Military Academy Archives)

CAPTAIN WILLIAM H. SAGE (USMA 1882).
Sage served at Fort Clark in the 23rd Infantry
from 1894–98, commanding Fort Clark's
"bicycle corps." He received the Medal of
Honor in 1902 in the Philippine Insurrection.
(U.S. Military Academy Archives)

Handwritten annotations on photograph:

Marateller 24 Inf.   Eggleston 10 Car.   Ellis 8 Car.   Guest 8 Car.
Paulding 10 Inf.   Pond 8 car.

SUBALTERNS, C. 1878. In one of the earliest photographs of soldiers at Fort Clark, these young Second Lieutenants are, from left to right: (front row) Robert H. R. Loughborough, 25th Infantry; Charles Judson Crane, 24th Infantry; Robert C. Van Vliet, 10th Infantry; (middle row) James S. Marteller, 24th Infantry; Eugene A. Ellis, 8th Cavalry; George E. Pond, 8th Cavalry; (back row) William Paulding, 10th Infantry; Millard F. Eggleston, 10th Cavalry; Frederick E. Phelps, 8th Cavalry; and John Guest Jr., 8th Cavalry. In his memoirs, 2nd Lieutenant Paulding describes the post as *"...one of great distances, three-quarters of a mile from the C.O.'s (Commanding Officer) quarters to the Q.M. (Quartermaster) store house and no shade ..."* Paulding's men nicknamed him "the kid" due to his youthful appearance. In the summer of 1875 Paulding ran the first telegraph line from Fort Clark to the Menger Hotel in San Antonio. (Photograph courtesy of Lawrence T. Jones III, Austin)

C. D. CURTIS,

FORT CLARK.
TEXAS.

U. S. ARMY PHOTOGRAPHER.

STUDIO CARD BY C.D. CURTIS, C. 1890s. In an age when smiling for the camera simply didn't happen, this young lady sat for her portrait. The ornate wicker seat is a typical studio prop of the period and the most popular furniture in the Army because it was lightweight and inexpensive. The photographer, C.D. Curtis, remains a rather elusive character. Many late 19th-century photographs of the fort bear his name, an identity as a "U.S. Army Photographer," and the location of "Fort Clark, Texas." This author does not know whether he was a soldier or simply worked for the Army as an official photographer. His timeless photographs of the fort and its inhabitants are of superb composition and quality, making him one of Fort Clark's unsung heroes. (Collection of Chris A. Hale)

27

TROOP F, 8TH CAVALRY 1885. The 8th Cavalry served at Fort Clark from 1876 until 1888. Pictured here is Troop "F" of the regiment with its complement of 3 officers and 37 enlisted men. The mounted troopers are carrying their sabers at present and wearing the white Model 1880 cork summer helmet and white gauntlets. The troop commander, a captain, is in front while his two lieutenants are off to the left on white horses. The troop guidon unfurls in the breeze. (Collection of Chris A. Hale)

LIEUTENANT GENERAL SAMUEL B.M. YOUNG, FIRST U.S. ARMY CHIEF OF STAFF. As a troop commander in the 8th Cavalry at Fort Clark 1877–78, then Captain Young was well known for his exploits in the region and for raids into Mexico, serving under both Colonel Mackenzie and Lieutenant Colonel Shafter. While at Fort Clark he also frequently campaigned with Lieutenant Bullis and the Seminole Scouts. Rising to the highest level of distinction in the Army, Young succeeded Nelson A. Miles in 1903 to become the last Commanding General of the U.S. Army. Six days later the position was abolished and Young became the first Chief of Staff of the United States Army. (Photo courtesy of Howard W. Hardy, Seattle, Washington, grandnephew of Lieutenant General Young)

FRANCIS HENRY FRENCH, IN HIS FULL DRESS UNIFORM AS A 1ST LIEUTENANT OF THE 19TH INFANTRY. French was born in Fort Wayne, Indiana, on September 27, 1857. Deeply impressed from his youth by the stirring deeds and stories told by veterans of the Civil War, he realized his ambition for a military career by entering the U.S. Military Academy at West Point, New York where he graduated 12th from the class of 1879. He was assigned as 2nd Lieutenant of "E" Company 19th Infantry and came west. Following service at Fort Garland, Colorado Territory, and Fort Leavenworth, Kansas, the regiment moved to Fort Brown at Brownsville, Texas, where Lieutenant French was detailed as the Regimental Adjutant. In December 1882 the 19th Infantry was posted to Fort Clark. At Fort Clark, on January 1, 1883, Lt French began diaries which he faithfully maintained for the next thirty years. The Fort Clark period of these diaries from 1883–1888 and his letters home are an intriguing window to late 19th century Army life at Fort Clark and to the American experience of the Victorian era. Lieutenant French's command of the famed Seminole Negro Indian Scouts is particularly noteworthy as the young officer developed a lifelong respect for the scouts as soldiers and men. He was a caring and sensitive man with opinions on people and politics. He was a bachelor immersed in the "society" of Fort Clark. However, always in the background was his profession of being a soldier and an officer, which he took quite seriously. (The Vinton Trust)

OFFICERS' LINE, C. 1880S. In the early 1870s Fort Clark rapidly expanded to accommodate and support the regimental size garrison needed to deal effectively with the increasing number of Indian depredations along the border. The post doubled in size from 1873 to 1875. The post surgeon reported, *"Nine new buildings are now completed for officers' quarters; they are built of stone, two stories high, with porch in front, and back buildings."* These quarters face the new parade ground and are aligned on an "L" shape axis with six sets on the long side of the "L," two sets on the short side, and then the Commanding Officer's Quarters (in the left distance). In this view, two officers stand in front of the neat line of picket fences, chinaberry trees, well-kept lawns, and porches with Madeira vines. The officer in white is thought to be Zenus R. Bliss then Lieutenant Colonel of the 19th Infantry. (National Archives)

MRS. INDA GUARD, C. 1882. Inda Guard was the wife of Alexander McCook Guard (USMA 1871), 1st Lieutenant of "E" Company, 19th Infantry. As a good army wife she saw to it that the junior bachelor officer of the company (Lieutenant French) behaved himself, had an occasional hearty meal, and participated in the "society" of the regiment. She is pictured twice more in the photos of *The Mikado* production. (The Vinton Trust)

BREVET MAJOR GENERAL CHARLES H. SMITH, IN FULL DRESS AS COLONEL OF THE 19TH INFANTRY. The 19th Infantry served at Fort Clark from 1882 until 1889. General Smith was a Civil War veteran awarded the Congressional Medal of Honor on April 11, 1895, for distinguished gallantry at St Mary's Church, Virginia, June 24, 1864. Lieutenant French wrote home in January of 1886 that, *"…Genl. Smith is making a great many improvements around the garrison which add materially to the appearance of the post as well as to the comfort of the people. Just now he is straightening and building up the roads, and putting new kitchens at the barracks and raising the officers kitchens one story."* This photograph was given to Lieutenant French by an orderly on the morning of June 15, 1886. The young lieutenant had great respect for his commander but often questioned his indecisiveness. As for the general, he felt there were a few gentlemen in the Army and Lieutenant French was one of them. (The Vinton Trust)

"LE CERCLE FRANCAIS." Shown is the porch of 1st Lieutenant and Mrs. Quincy Gillmore's quarters (No. 14), Monday afternoon, April 26, 1886. This group of officers and ladies formed a club in November 1885 to teach each other to read and speak French. They met each Tuesday evening at the Gillmore quarters. Their last meeting took place the next night—the group temporarily disbanded due to the departure of Mrs. Gillmore. Officers standing from left are: Lieutenant Hammond, "L" Troop 8th Cavalry; Captain Vance, "E" Co. 19th Infantry; 1st Lt. Henry F. Kendall (USMA 1878), "E" Troop 8th Cavalry; and Lieutenant French. Officers seated from left are: Lieutenant Hewitt, "C" Co. 19th Infantry; and Major Francis Laban Town, Post Surgeon. Although they cannot be specifically identified, the ladies are Mrs. Gillmore, Mrs. Lyster, Mrs. Hall, and Miss Saunders. (The Vinton Trust)

CAPTAIN RICHARD VANCE. A grizzled Civil War veteran with distinctive mutton chop sideburns who served in the 19th Infantry for 24 years, Vance never rose above the rank of captain. He was Lieutenant French's company commander. A skilled trainer, he schooled the young lieutenant in the practical methods of soldiering not taught at West Point. He was also a reliable source of loans when funds ran out before payday. (The Vinton Trust)-

1ST LIEUTENANT CHRISTIAN CYRUS HEWITT (USMA 1874). Hewitt was assigned to the 19th Infantry upon his graduation from West Point in 1874 and served in the regiment until he retired as a major in 1901. He and French were close friends during their time together at Fort Clark. The two competed for the attention of a succession of young ladies, played daily games of billiards at the sutler's store, and sought infrequent exercise by playing tennis matches. On his collar Lieutenant Hewitt is wearing the Marksmanship Badges he earned on Fort Clark's rifle range. (The Vinton Trust)

"LE CERCLE FRANCAIS." From Lieutenant French's diary, April 26, 1886, "*Had charge of the company at dress parade, Capt. Vance not going out. Before studying French, the Cercle Francais met at Mrs. Gillmore's and had two pictures taken. Hope these will be good as want good pictures of the club.*" In this second photograph the ladies have not moved but the officers have changed position. The reader may easily identify the officers, particularly Captain Vance in his straw hat. Quarters No. 14–15 turned out to be the location of the picture as it is the only set of quarters with a six-light transom. (The Vinton Trust)

33

LIEUTENANT FRENCH'S QUARTERS AND "THE OFFICE," C. 1885. Lieutenant French sent this postcard home in November of 1885. The building on the left is quarters No. 6–7. French occupied the right set with another bachelor officer in 1883–84. The right-hand building is the Post Headquarters, or "the office" as French referred to it. The Post Hospital is in the distance between the two buildings. A mule-drawn wagon is in the foreground. (Fort Clark Historical Society)

THE MIKADO CAST, 1887. Officers and ladies of the 19th Infantry and 8th Cavalry perform *The Mikado* at the post hall, February 8 and 11, 1887. Lieutenant Hammond and Mrs. Hammond are looking at each other far left, Mrs. Guard is center rear, Miss Jordan is the third lady from the right, and Lieutenant French is on the far right. Other players are not identified. The company rehearsed the Gilbert and Sullivan operetta (which first opened at London's Savoy Theater in 1885) for weeks and held just two performances, the second of which, according to Lieutenant French's diary, *"… the audience was much more liberal in praise and on the whole I think the opera was much more successfully given."* (The Vinton Trust)

34

"THREE LITTLE MAIDS FROM SCHOOL ARE WE ..." Pictured, from left, are Mrs. Hammond, wife of Lieutenant Andrew Goodrich Hammond (USMA 1881) 8th Cavalry, as Peep-Bo; Mrs. Inda Guard as Yum-Yum; and Miss Jordan, the post schoolteacher, as Pitti-Sing. The effort these ladies put into their performance is obvious. For at least two nights in February of 1887 the frontier post experienced the high society and elegance of the London stage. Lieutenant French's diary entry from the first performance is worth sharing here, *"Cut off moustache after dinner and put on cit clothes and then went to Mrs. Guard's who fixed my hair and face for the opera. This is the first time have shaved off moustache since leaving West Point; feel strange without it. After finishing at Mrs. Guard's went over to Library and dressed there and then took the part of Nanki Poo in the opera of the "Mikado." Made a few trifling errors but got through without any serious mistake. Ives & Guard forgot a little of their songs but the thing was a grand success on the whole. Everybody in the audience was pleased. Expected to be very much frightened but did not feel so at all. Am very glad it was so successful. They want to have another performance soon. Dressed at the Library leaving clothes over there in case of another performance and walked back with Guard and wife, both of whom did very well. The honors lay with Miss Coleman and Guard. Was very glad that the former did so well as she has worked very hard. Hewitt called after the performance and was quite complimentary. Had to work a long time afterwards to get the paint off my face and head."* (The Vinton Trust)

INSPECTION OF REGIMENT IN CAMP, C. 1896. Infantrymen of the 23rd Infantry Regiment stand inspection in front of their shelter tents in this view taken to the southwest of the post (main post is visible in the upper left distance). Inspecting officers move down the line of tents. In the center of the photo the Regimental colors are furled and laying between two stacks of rifles under the watchful eye of the Sergeant Major, and a lady sits in a carriage observing the proceedings. A fighting trench is visible in the foreground. The hospital tent, which appears in another photo, is in the right distance. (Robert J. Sporleder Album, Fort Clark Historical Society)

ERECTING HASTY ENTRENCHMENTS, C. 1896. An officer stares at the camera over the breastworks, while another places his hand on the sandbagged revetment, as the same soldiers who were standing inspection in the photo above now dig a line of hasty entrenchments. On the right of the picture a bugler watches two NCOs digging. A company of soldiers waits their turn to the left of the mounted officer. The tent camp is in the distance. (Robert J. Sporleder Album, Fort Clark Historical Society)

COMPANY OF INFANTRY DEFENDING BREASTWORKS, C. 1896. With their captain, lieutenant, and buglers looking on, a company of the 23rd Infantry Regiment mounts the firing step of their sandbag-reinforced breastwork. The soldiers are armed with Model 1892 30–40 caliber Krag-Jorgensen rifles and are all wearing *c.* 1894 double row Mills cartridge belts. The company First Sergeant is the second soldier from the right. There are two dogs in the picture—one at the end of the trench and one near the tent. Judging from the trees, the site may be near the spring. (Robert J. Sporleder Album, Fort Clark Historical Society)

MILITARY FUNERAL, C. 1896. A cavalryman is put to rest in the post cemetery. Soldiers stand at parade rest in their white helmets and duck trousers wearing the sabers, which identify them as cavalrymen. Ladies with umbrellas are at the far left. The moment may be best described by a similar event from Lieutenant French's diary, "... *attended the funeral of Pvt. Reith, "E" Co., 19th Inf'y, Capt. Vance, Guard & I being chief mourners, in full dress walking just after the corpse. Reith was very popular and was a very deserving man. He died suddenly yesterday, the autopsy today revealing a perforation of the intestines due to typhoid fever. The ceremony was quite impressive, especially the sounding of taps after the salute had been fired.*" (Robert J. Sporleder Album, Fort Clark Historical Society)

POST OFFICE, C. 1891. View of soldiers and citizens mingling on Ann Street outside a dominant Brackettville building, which then served as the first post office and county courthouse. The presence of the Army in the community is very evident in this photo. The building was erected in the early 1870s and is still in use today, minus its second story, as the office of *The Brackett News*. (Zack Davis Collection)

STAGE TO SPOFFORD, C. 1880S. When the Southern Pacific Railroad bypassed Brackettville in 1882, a stage line was started to transport passengers from Brackettville the nine miles south to the railhead at Spofford. This "stagecoach" looks suspiciously like a surplus Army ambulance. The coach, with paying customers aboard, is on Spring Street pointed in the direction of Spofford, a soldier on horseback stares at the camera, while men and dogs strike a pose. The post office on Ann Street is in the background. (Zack Davis Collection)

VIEW OF ANN STREET LOOKING NORTH TOWARDS LAS MORAS MOUNTAIN, C. 1890S. The post office is on the left (now *Brackett News* building) and further on is the building that is now the Masonic Lodge. Prominent citizens gather in the street for the photographer whose wagon is in the right foreground under boot maker A. Studer's sign. Further down the street on the right is the county jail and in the distance the schoolhouse. (Zack Davis Collection)

COCKFIGHT IN BRACKETT DECEMBER 15, 1889. Soldiers, townsfolk, and a makeshift band look on as the festivities are about to begin. The referee has his thumb on the hammer of his pistol, two boys are set to release their fighting cocks, while the next contestants in the ring are fitted with spurs, and several contenders strut on the railing. In the back of the crowd a number of hopefuls hold up their roosters for the camera. (Zack Davis Collection)

CORNER OF ANN AND SPRING STREETS, C. 1896. This intersection, known locally as "Five Points," is the subject of dozens of photographs. Ann Street, named for Ann Ross, a pioneer resident of Brackettville, stretches north towards Las Moras Mountain in the distance. The building in the left foreground, then a store, later became the First State Bank. A barber pole is clearly visible up the street on the right. Although there are none in the picture, evidence of horses is present. (Robert J. Sporleder Album, Fort Clark Historical Society)

KINNEY COUNTY JAIL, C. 1885. This imposing structure is one of the finest stone buildings ever constructed in Kinney County. Texas is very proud of her jails and Kinney County was no exception. Some of the men in this photo have the look of desperados who should be inside instead of outside. The second story of the building was removed in the 1920s because of structural damage from a series of disastrous floods. The building now serves as the Kinney County Nutrition Center. (Zack Davis Collection)

SNOWSTORM IN BRACKETT, 1897. This view of Brackettville, blanketed in snow, looking north towards Las Moras Mountain, was taken from atop the windmill on the Roach Company property. The "Blacksmith" building is on Ann Street; to its left is the livery and Las Moras Stage Co. featured in the photo on page 38. Upper left is the county jail that fronts on Ann Street. The Episcopal Church is on the upper right. (Zack Davis Collection)

VELTMANN & SON STORE, C. 1890S. Joseph Veltmann's store was on the corner across from the buildings on Ann Street in the top photo on the opposite page. Mr. Veltmann is described as an enterprising businessman who held large contracts with the Army to supply wood to Fort Clark. The early photos of Brackettville all seem to feature an abundance of idle men posing for the camera. The building still stands and was most recently the office of Mr. Sterling Evans. (Zack Davis Collection)

41

BRACKETTVILLE "BUSINESS DISTRICT," C. 1900. This is the corner of Ann and Spring Streets at the turn of the century. Saloons flourished in downtown Brackett thanks to a devoted clientele of soldiers. By the 1930s the corner building had become McCabe's drug store. Down the east side of Ann Street is a line of businesses, private homes, and on the end, the county jail. The Las Moras Stage Co. is the building on the right edge of the photograph. (Zack Davis Collection)

"OXIEN BASE-BALL NINE" BRACKETT, TEXAS, OCTOBER, 1891. Since not one of these gentlemen can be identified, perhaps they are a barnstorming team typical of the era come to challenge the local "nine!" Regardless of their origins or allegiances they are baseball players from the first golden age of baseball, the 1890s. Officer's diaries and memoirs never fail to mention the distraction of baseball as one of the only pastimes that kept the soldiers out of the "rum-holes" in Brackettville. (Zack Davis Collection)

FIRST POST COMMISSARY, C. 1880S. An essential building on every post, the Commissary was under the purview of the Regimental or Post Quartermaster and served as a storehouse and distribution point for foodstuffs and rations. Seminole Hall, a two-story stone barracks built in 1932, now occupies the site. The post butcher shop is behind the building on the left of the photo. (National Archives)

NEW QUARTERMASTER STOREHOUSE, 1892. This massive building, the largest on the post, was constructed in 1892 of ashlar limestone and contains over 15,000 square feet of warehouse space. In this early view, the building is naturally illuminated by the setting sun and the full gallery porches, seen in subsequent photos, are not present. (Collection of Chris A. Hale)

DETACHMENT OF INFANTRY IN HEAVY MARCHING ORDER, 1896. These soldiers are from "G" Company 23rd Infantry, the unit designation stenciled on the haversack of the fourth soldier from the left. The Regiment served at Fort Clark 1894–1898. The corporal on the left is wearing his Marksman pins on his collar. Heavy marching order includes: Model 1892 30–40 caliber Krag-Jorgensen rifle; double row Mills cartridge belt; canteen, haversack, and bayonet; and a full pack with shelter half and blanket roll. Mustaches and pipes are optional. (Robert J. Sporleder Album, Fort Clark Historical Society)

INFANTRY BARRACKS PREPARED FOR INSPECTION, C. 1896. Anyone who has ever been a soldier is familiar with this scene. The barracks is spotless, footlockers open with every item in its designated place, bunks, headgear, blankets, sheets, each soldiers' worldly possessions, "dressed right and covered down!" The photo was taken when the morning sun filled the room. This is one of the six single-story infantry barracks. Note the iron stoves, rifle rack, and Model 1891 two-burner barracks lamp down the center of the room. (Robert J. Sporleder Album, Fort Clark Historical Society)

POST GUARDHOUSE, C. 1896. A lone sentinel of the guard stands at attention in his white helmet and white duck trousers, while his fellow soldiers gather on the porch. The guardhouse was finished in 1874 as part of the expansion of the post. This building was the heartbeat of the garrison, as it never closed. Most soldiers who served at Fort Clark experienced this building while on guard duty or more unluckily as a prisoner. In the center of the picture is a caisson, further left a field piece, and the square building to the rear is a company sink or latrine. (Robert J. Sporleder Album, Fort Clark Historical Society)

POST GYMNASIUM, C. 1896. As the 19th century drew to a close, the Army made a conscious effort to get in step with American society by providing the soldiers with modern recreation facilities. At Fort Clark an infantry barracks was converted to a gymnasium, complete with rings and walls lined with medicine clubs. In the foreground a soldier sits in the rings, while two soldiers box, and two others fence at the end of the room. As in most gymnasiums, spectators abound. (Robert J. Sporleder Album, Fort Clark Historical Society)

POST FOOTBRIDGE, C. 1896. Two soldiers stare into Las Moras creek on the footbridge used by generations of soldiers to leave the fort and go to Brackettville. The fort is on the high ground up the stairs, which end behind the Quartermaster Storehouse (now the site of Las Moras Restaurant). Note the turnstile on the Brackettville end of the bridge. This bridge was still in service as late as 1928. (Robert J. Sporleder Album, Fort Clark Historical Society)

WAGON BRIDGE UNDER CONSTRUCTION, C. 1888. Soldiers look on as stonemasons complete another pier for the wagon bridge across Las Moras creek. A stone held by iron tongs is moved into position by a simple wooden crane under the watchful eye of an engineer. One of the two-story barracks can be seen in the background. This bridge was replaced in 1937 by a new bridge built by the W.P.A., which is still in use. (Zack Davis Collection)

A TOAST TO THE CAMERA, C. 1880S. The truth be known, soldiers drink! They also on occasion chase women. Both pursuits were fulfilled just across Las Moras creek in Brackettville. Too often relief from the tedium of soldiering was found in a bottle. This group of 8th Cavalry troopers is in the photographer's studio rejoicing in their favorite pastime. The soldier seated on the left may be a farrier, judging from his apron and hammer. (Collection of Chris A. Hale)

BLANKET TOSS, C. 1890S. Carrying on a tradition as old as the Army, a new recruit is welcomed to the regiment by being repeatedly tossed high into the air by his fellow soldiers using a blanket like a trampoline. The picture on page 90 shows the 1930s version of this same initiation rite. (Fort Clark Historical Society)

47

LAUNDRESSES ON LAS MORAS CREEK, C. 1898. Laundry hangs in the trees while laundresses and their children temporary halt from their drudgery for the photographer. The lady in the center holds a baby, and a group of little girls share the workload. Army laundresses were typically the wives of non-commissioned officers and lived in an area behind barracks row commonly referred to as "Sudsville." The Army sanctioned their presence on the post and each unit was allocated funds to pay these ladies for the cleaning of the soldier's uniforms. The soldier on the right, with the white horse, may be a Seminole Scout. The saddle is civilian, not military. The reader may study the photo of the scouts mounted (page 63) and reach your own conclusion. (Collection of Chris A. Hale)

POST BANDSTAND, C. 1880S. The focal point for evening concerts by the Regimental band, and prominently located in front of the Commanding Officer's quarters, this decidedly Victorian structure is in many photographs of the parade ground. The present day bandstand was reconstructed in 1993, from this photo. On January 3, 1883, Lieutenant French wrote, *"...Marie and I went out for a stroll and then the dear, dear girl told me something that made me exceedingly happy. I shall always retain a great liking for the music stand on the parade at Fort Clark."* (National Archives)

CAPTAIN CHARLES M. GANDY. A Medical Corps officer, Captain Gandy served as Fort Clark's Assistant Post Surgeon in the early 1890s. His hobby was photography, and this image may indeed be a self-portrait. Five of the photographs he made of his quarters and his daughter are included in this chapter. Gandy and Lieutenant French were acquaintances when they served together at Fort Concho in San Angelo, Texas. The small bar on his tunic is his Marksman badge, a distinction not normally achieved by Medical Corps officers. (William Hilderbrand, Gainesville, Texas from glass negative)

POST HOSPITAL, C. 1896. This building was completed in 1874, replacing an earlier hospital, which then became the band barracks. This facility is typical of hospitals on frontier posts with a central two-story administration building and two single-story wings to serve as patient wards, each accommodating eight beds. It was the largest building on the post until 1892 when the new commissary was constructed. The cupola on the rooftop was the vantage point for many early panoramic photographs of the garrison. Note the tin roof (probably red) and the soldier patients on the porch, which completely encircled the building. A white picket fence kept out animals. (Robert J. Sporleder Album, Fort Clark Historical Society)

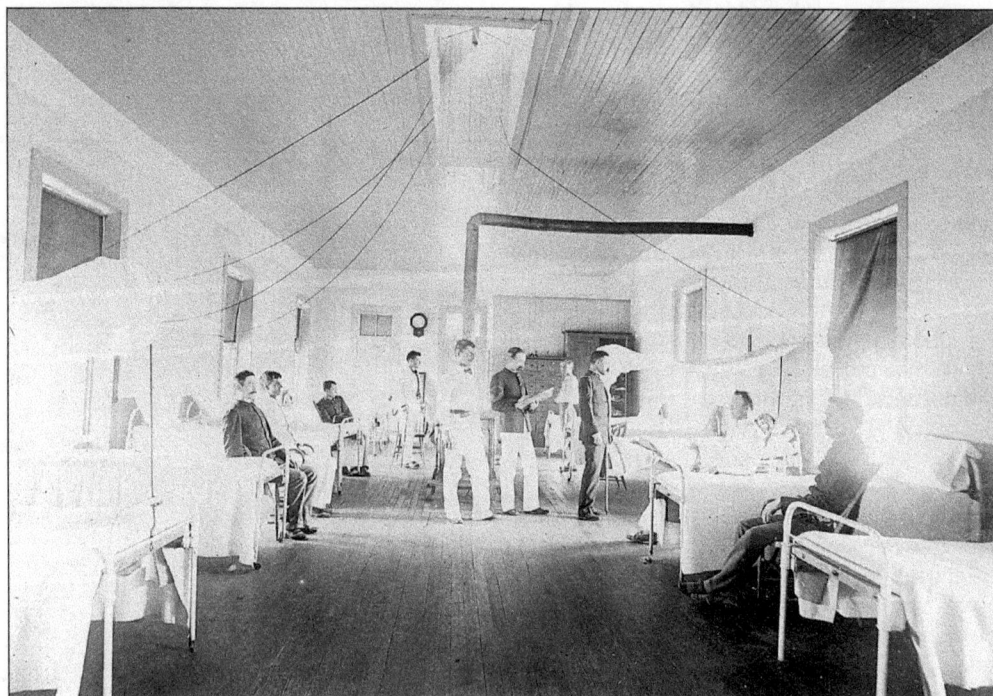

POST HOSPITAL WARD, C. 1896. The Assistant Post Surgeon, Capt. Charles M. Gandy (officer standing right center) conducts sick call, while the enlisted hospital steward (sergeant behind the surgeon, with ledger book) records the observations. The airy sunlit room, complete with roof vent and mosquito netting, was intended to promote speedy recovery. (Robert J. Sporleder Album, Fort Clark Historical Society)

MEDICAL CORPS FIELD TRAINING, C. 1896. This is a superb photograph of the U.S. Army's "Improved Ambulance, 1892 pattern" in action. Stretcher-bearers move a patient, who is sitting up to see where he's going, to the hospital tent in this field training exercise, which took place in plain view of the post. Note the bicycle in the mesquite brush next to the tent. (Robert J. Sporleder Album, Fort Clark Historical Society)

SNOWSTORM, NOVEMBER 30, 1896. Two soldiers in overcoats, a corporal, and a boy move across the parade ground in a snowstorm, towards the officers' line of quarters. Snow is a rare occurrence in south Texas so this must have been a memorable experience for the garrison. For the soldiers in the barracks warm around their stoves, it meant there would be no parade! (Robert J. Sporleder Album, Fort Clark Historical Society)

CAPTAIN GANDY'S QUARTERS ON "THE LINE," C. 1895. Capt. Charles M. Gandy, the Assistant Post Surgeon, whose hobby was photography, took the next five photographs. Gandy and his family lived in Quarters No. 17. In this view looking northeast the neat line of picket fences and chinaberry trees is interrupted by a little girl, Gandy's daughter Lila, standing at the gate to her home. A neighbor looks on from his yard. Note the bent tree in front of the porch, the hammock on the porch, the cart by the side window, and the off-color stone at the upper left of the window which helped identify the building. (William Hilderbrand, Gainesville, Texas, from glass negative)

QUARTERS NO. 16–17, C. 1895. Eight sets of limestone duplex officers' quarters were completed in 1873–74. The kitchens were raised one story in 1886. Each set of quarters contains almost 3,000 square feet of living space. Again the cart and bent tree on Captain Gandy's side are plainly visible. These buildings have changed little in 128 years. They are still enjoyed and cared for by their current occupants. Yet I think somehow even now footsteps echo from the countless Army families who made these houses their homes. (William Hilderbrand, Gainesville, Texas, from glass negative)

CARRIAGE AT GATE TO GANDY QUARTERS, C. 1895. Lila Gandy and horses Montana and Yellowstone patiently wait for father to take the picture so they can go for a carriage ride. Behind the carriage is the parade ground and enlisted barracks. These gates often defined social behavior as Lieutenant French noted on March 21, 1886: "*Capt. Vance took retreat for me. Returning Capt. Hall went past his wife and deliberately walked up on Mrs. Feche't's porch and commenced to talk to her, leaving Mrs. Hall standing down by the next gate. Mrs. Hall blushed scarlet and seemed very much annoyed. Capt. Hall isn't good enough for his wife and doesn't deserve such a true woman as Mrs.*" (William Hilderbrand, Gainesville, Texas, from glass negative)

DOWN "THE LINE," C. 1895. If you have ever taken a picture of your home you can appreciate Captain Gandy's fascination for his. Again the bent tree, picket fences between quarters, a boot scraper, shutters on the windows, Madeira vines on the porches (the fragrance helped keep insects away), and a chinaberry tree. At the far end of the line a woman is watering her flowers. (William Hilderbrand, Gainesville, Texas, from glass negative)

53

FRONT PORCH OF CAPTAIN GANDY'S QUARTERS. Lila Gandy is sound asleep in the hammock on the porch of the family's quarters, while her father and mother gently rock the hammock from either end. The bent tree pointed out in previous photos is plainly visible in front of the porch. (William Hilderbrand, Gainesville, Texas, from glass negative)

DRESS PARADE, C. 1880S. This excerpt is from Lieutenant French's diary, Monday, May 17, 1886: *"Had parade in white helmets tonight. The wind came up suddenly from the North and sent some of the helmets flying."* The perceived monotony of military life was punctuated by the daily dress parade. Seven days a week, week in and week out, with relief coming only when it was too hot or too cold, the soldiers stood on the parade ground for the lowering of the colors at retreat. Pictured here on parade are nine companies of an infantry regiment, a single officer in front of each company, and NCOs to the rear. The post hospital is in background and an ambulance sits beyond the far end of the line. (William Hilderbrand, Gainesville, Texas, from glass negative)

OFFICERS AND LADIES TENNIS MATCH, C. 1889. Tennis was a very popular pastime for Army society by the 1880s. Identified from left are: Lieutenant William T. Oliver of the 19th Infantry, Willie Jordon, Mary Leefe (17-year-old daughter of Capt. John G. Leefe, 19th Infantry), Sax Pope, Chuck Leefe, Will Washington (in tree), Issa Jordon, Miss Purington, Miss McKee, and Asst. Surgeon Lt. Ogden Rafferty. The new staff officers' quarters, with second-floor veranda, completed in 1888, stands prominently in the left background (the Patton House). A tennis court still occupies this site. (Fort Clark Historical Society)

CAMP LIFE, C. 1880S. If a picture is worth a thousand words, this is the one! Judging from the size of the trees and plants, this Army escort wagon is somewhere near Las Moras creek. The clutter of the camp is considerable. Pots and pans hanging in the trees, carbines and cartridge belts leaning against the trees, an axe stuck in a tree, dutch ovens on the fire, a stack of biscuits and a coffee grinder on the barrel heads, army blankets draped on the wagon, five mules, three characters who may be teamsters or possibly army cooks, and one tired dog, who could care less!(Texas Museum of Military History)

PRACTICE MARCH, C. 1895. After crossing the wagon bridge over Las Moras creek and entering Fort Clark, Captain Lea Febiger (bearded officer with eyeglasses and saber, behind the drummer) halts two companies of the 23rd Infantry to pose for U.S. Army photographer C.D. Curtis. The infantry column is returning from a practice march to the East Nueces River in October 1895. The event was covered by Harpers Weekly correspondent/artist Frederic Remington who drew A Practice March in Texas, for the nationally syndicated periodical. (Collection of Chris A. Hale)

A PRACTICE MARCH IN TEXAS DRAWN BY FREDERIC REMINGTON. The article and drawing appeared in the January 4, 1896, issue of Harper's. Remington quoted Captain Febiger as reporting, "There were numerous complaints of the government shoe, and they wore much worse than those purchased outside. The new shelter-tent with the elongated rear end was very satisfactory, except that it is far from rain-proof in anything like a heavy shower." Remington added, "Indeed, no tent is proof for that matter." (Courtesy Frederic Remington Art Museum, Ogdensburg, New York)

56

The Soldier's Standard Bicycle.

PARTS MADE ON INTERCHANGEABLE SYSTEM,

Of the best materials, and thoroughly tested by skilled workmen.

Columbia Light Roadster.

The only cycle used in regular military service in the Army. Made by the oldest, largest, and best makers of bicycles in the United States, the

POPE MANUFACTURING CO.

GENERAL OFFICES AND WAREROOMS,
221 COLUMBUS AVENUE, BOSTON, MASS.

BRANCH OFFICES, 12 WARREN ST., NEW YORK, N. Y.
291 WABASH AVE., CHICAGO, ILL.

Agents throughout the country.

Factories, Hartford, Conn.

THE SOLDIER'S STANDARD BICYCLE, 1892.
This advertisement is from the "Cycle-Infantry Drill Regulations" prepared by Brig. Gen. Albert Ordway and adopted March 25, 1892. The tiny manual was actually published by the Pope Manufacturing Company to foster use of their bicycle by the Army. With the Army's Commanding General Nelson A. Miles fully supporting and encouraging military bicycle use, any post with an Infantry garrison was caught up in the bicycle trials. Fort Clark, as home to the 23rd Infantry since June 1894, was logically a candidate for bicycle experimentation. The *Post Returns* of October 1895 document the beginnings of Fort Clark's experience with the bicycle. Captain Febiger's orders for his practice march from Col. Samuel Ovenshine, commander of the 23rd Infantry and Fort Clark, contained the provision for bicycle participation, *"the command not having transportation of any kind on the march, should it become necessary to communicate with the post for any purpose whatever, may do so by bicycles, the use of which on the march by enlisted men owning them is hereby authorized."* (Author's collection)

57

PANORAMIC VIEWS OF FORT CLARK, 1898. The next four photographs capture a 360-degree view of the post at the end of the 19th century. The camera position is on the old parade ground. The deserted appearance of the fort cannot be explained. In 1898, the 23rd Infantry departed and the 3rd Texas Infantry arrived to garrison the fort for the duration of the Spanish-American War. Perhaps there was a lull between those two events. Pictured from left are

PANORAMIC VIEW OF FORT CLARK, 1898. Pictured from left are the Company supply and administration (orderly room) building, now a private home; two-story cavalry barracks built in 1873–4, rebuilt in 1931, now Patton Hall motel; another two-story cavalry barracks built in

the original post hospital built in the 1850s and subsequently used as the band barracks (the building was torn down in the 1930s); Las Moras Mountain; Quartermaster Storehouse, also built in the 1850s (the Officers' Club was built on this site in 1939); post bakery; and the two-story cavalry barracks built in 1873–74, rebuilt in 1931, and currently Member Services for the Fort Clark Springs Association. (Collection of Chris A. Hale)

1873–4, rebuilt in 1932, now Bullis Hall motel; the old commissary (see photo on page 43); Quartermaster workshops new in 1892, now private homes; new commissary (see photo page 43); guardhouse; and infantry barracks. (Collection of Chris A. Hale)

PANORAMIC VIEW OF FORT CLARK, 1898. Pictured from left are a line of infantry barracks built 1870–74, now private homes; post hospital; post flagpole, which has had several different locations over time (note gas street light to right of pole); hose house where fire fighting equipment was stored, now site of the Post Theater; Post Commander's quarters with bandstand

PANORAMIC VIEW OF FORT CLARK, 1898. Pictured from left are the Post Headquarters completed in 1857 (see photo on page 17); staff officers' quarters No. 25–26 (the author's home is the right side); "the line" of two-story officers' quarters with double chimneys, now all private homes; sentry box; quarters No. 8–9 with hip roof, built in 1870; top of 1895 wooden water tower; hidden by trees behind the picket fence are quarters No. 2–3 and No. 4 which

in front; staff officers' quarters No. 27–28 (see page 108); and officers' duplex quarters No. 6–7 built in 1870 (Lieutenant French occupied the right side set in 1883–84), now a private home. (Collection of Chris A. Hale)

were put up in 1854 and are of horizontal log and vertical post construction, still occupied as private residences; and Bachelor Hall opened in October 1885 with Lieutenant French as one of the first eight occupants. The building contains eight two-room apartments, and Lieutenant French's set was on the second floor. He watched baseball games from his porch; the building is now the Cavalryman Condominiums. (Collection of Chris A. Hale)

ROACH & CO. BUILDING, C. 1900. Established in 1877 as Roach & Mahon, the business was succeeded by Roach & Co. as noted on the sign in this image. The windmill behind the building was used to take the photo on page 41. This building housed the largest general merchandise store in Kinney County and prospered from Fort Clark's business. In this view the building is draped in mourning for the passing of Mr. Roach. The garrison size flag could have only come from Fort Clark. (Zack Davis Collection)

PETERSEN & CO. BUILDING, C. 1903. Mr. N.P. Petersen was an employee of Henry Roach and was taken in as a partner in 1894. When Mr. Roach died, Petersen continued the thriving business under his name. A look inside proves Mr. Petersen was true to his slogan of selling "A Little of Everything." The shoeshine box in the far left doorway almost certainly belongs to the boy on the left. (Zack Davis Collection)

Four

THE SEMINOLE SCOUTS
FORT CLARK'S
MOST HEROIC UNIT

SEMINOLE-NEGRO INDIAN SCOUT DETACHMENT, FORT CLARK, TEXAS, JULY 1888. The front rank, left, is Sgt. Robert Kibbetts, one of the original scouts who served for 35 years from 1870 to 1905; and Cpl. Julian Longorio. The next rank, far left, is trumpeter Isaac Payne, a Medal of Honor recipient from the Bullis fight; Cpl. Joe Remo; Henry Washington; Ben July, who later became First Sergeant of the Detachment; Bill Williams; John July; Archibald Shields, who may be pictured with laundresses on page 48; William Shields; and Sandy Fay, who was Lt. Bullis's striker. Scouts in the rear rank, from left to right, are Medal of Honor recipient John Ward, who rescued Bullis; Antonio Sanches; Joe Dixon; Alfred Washington; Luce Cassas; Enrique Ortiz; and Ben Wilson, the Detachment farrier. These are the scouts Lieutenant French commanded at Meyers Spring, in February 1883, where he observed, *"I made them all wear the uniform as much as they could out here. Most of them have fine forms and are all strong healthy men. With proper drill, I think they would make a very military appearance."* French was so deeply moved by the scouts as soldiers and men, he ultimately referred to them as "my old warriors." (Autry Museum of Western Heritage, Los Angeles, In Memory of Sharon Johnson)

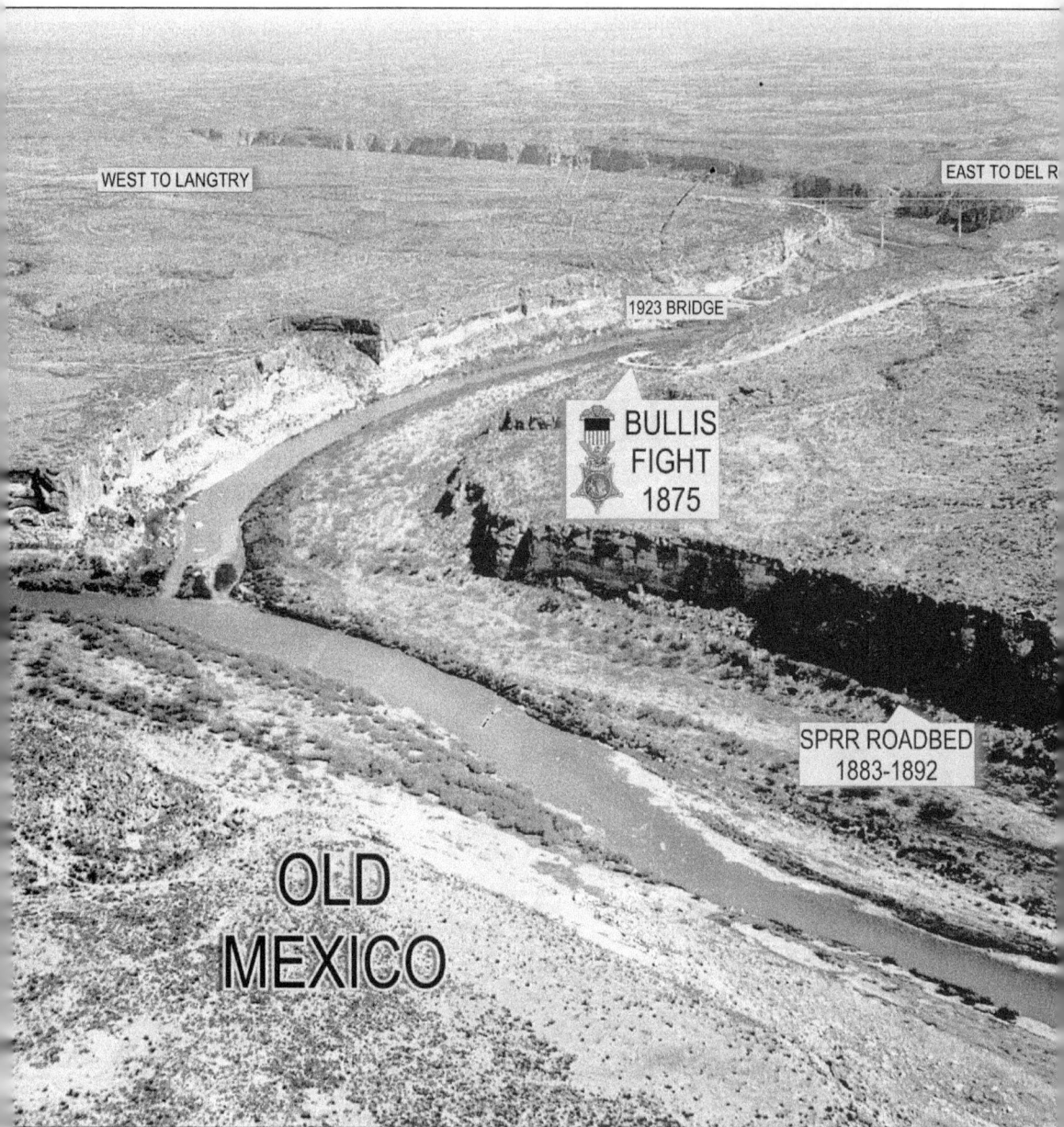

WEST TO LANGTRY

EAST TO DEL R

1923 BRIDGE

BULLIS
FIGHT
1875

SPRR ROADBED
1883-1892

OLD
MEXICO

MOUTH OF THE PECOS RIVER. The final 80 miles of the Pecos River's journey to the Rio Grande is the most formidable natural obstacle in Texas. This photograph, taken by Jim Zintgraff in 1962, captures the essence of a place that has been a crucible of human endeavor since man first entered these canyons some 12,000 years ago. In addition to the features and locations noted on the photograph, there are the living shelters of ancient Texan hunter gatherers and sites containing the finest rock art images in the New World. This place was familiar to Fort Clark's soldiers whether they crossed on Bullis's first road in the 1870s, on the railroad in the 1880s, or in a mounted column in the 1930s. Today, travelers on U.S. Hwy. 90 cross the Pecos with little effort on the highest highway bridge in Texas, not realizing the history they are passing through or the heroic efforts that made their crossing possible. (Photo courtesy of James W. Zintgraff)

LIEUTENANT JOHN LAPNAM BULLIS, C. 1870S. A native New Yorker, Bullis entered the service of his country as a corporal in Company H, 126th New York Infantry on August 8, 1862. By the end of the Civil War he was a captain in the 118th U.S. Colored Infantry, his first experience in command of Black soldiers. After the war he headed west and following several failed business enterprises reentered the Army in September of 1867 as a 2nd Lieutenant in the 41st Infantry, one of the newly formed Black regiments. The 41st Infantry arrived at Fort Clark in 1868 with Col. Ranald S. Mackenzie in command and William R. Shafter as his lieutenant colonel. In November 1869 the 41st was combined with the 38th Infantry to form the 24th Infantry (Buffalo Soldiers). Bullis took command of the Seminole-Negro Indian Scout Detachment in the Spring of 1872 when the scouts and their families moved to Fort Clark from Fort Duncan (Eagle Pass). His exploits as commander of the scouts are the stuff of legend. Bullis and the Scouts were the vanguard for Mackenzie's Remilino Raid in 1873 and participated in subsequent raids into Mexico with "Pecos Bill" Shafter and S.B.M. Young. Bullis relinquished command of the scouts in July of 1881. His singularly heroic service was recognized by gifts from the citizens of west Texas and of Kinney County of gold-plated and engraved presentation swords now held by the Witte Museum. Bullis retired from active service as a major and was promoted to brigadier general on the retired list just prior to his death at Fort Sam Houston in 1911. (Fort Clark Historical Society)

"SAVING THE LIEUTENANT'S HAIR" BY DALE GALLON. Based on Bullis's official report of the engagement and achieving remarkable historical accuracy, this painting is the first in the "Medal of Honor" series. The Pecos River Fight on April 25, 1875, during which Bullis was rescued by three of his faithful scouts, resulted in the award of the Medal of Honor to scouts Sgt. John Ward, Pvt. Pompey Factor, and trumpeter Isaac Payne (all buried in the Seminole Indian Scout Cemetery, Brackettville, Texas). (Courtesy of Gallon Historical Art, Gettysburg, Pennsylvania, 17325, www.gallon.com)

THE SEMINOLE CAMP ON FORT CLARK, C. 1896. A Seminole settlement was established on Fort Clark in 1872. The scouts and their families lived along the course of Las Moras Creek, some two miles south of the main post garrison. They referred to their simple jacal-thatched roofed homes as "the camp." Of his first visit there in May 1883, French wrote, *"Rode all around camp with Sgt. Kibbets and saw where the animals graze and where the men live. Some of them keep their places in nice condition all the time while others live like pigs."* These men and children are unidentified. A bedstead leans against the house on the left and a saddle hangs under the arbor. (Robert J. Sporleder Album, Fort Clark Historical Society)

SEMINOLE SCOUT GROUP, JANUARY 15, 1889. This photo was taken in Brackettville, possibly in front of the Filippone Store (now the home of the Kinney County Historical Commission) where the scouts had accounts. Pictured from left are Plantz Payne, Billy July, Ben July, Dembo Factor, Ben Wilson, John July, and William Shields. The July's are all brothers; their father, Sampson July, had also been a scout. Dembo Factor, who fought against the U.S. Army in the Second Seminole War in Florida in 1835, first enlisted as a scout at age 62 and served four years. (Courtesy of William "Dub" Warrior)

SCOUTS FAY JULY AND WILLIAM SHIELDS, C. 1894. Fay July, on the left, a corporal in this photo, was a scout for 21 years from 1893 until 1914. He was briefly the unit first sergeant and was discharged when the detachment was disbanded in the summer of 1914. William Shields enlisted as a scout at age 21 in January 1888 and served 20 years before he was discharged for disability in September 1908. (Courtesy of William "Dub" Warrior)

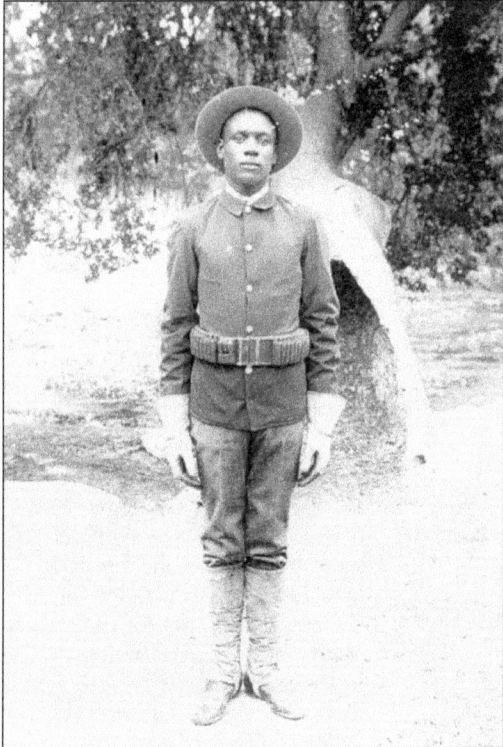

PRIVATE JOHN JEFFERSON, 10TH CAVALRY, C. 1890S. John Jefferson was born in the Seminole camp on Fort Clark in 1877, the grandson of Seminole-Negro patriarch John Horse. When he came of age he joined the regular Army and the Buffalo Soldiers of the 10th Cavalry. His Seminole roots brought him back to Fort Clark in the spring of 1905, where he enlisted in the scouts. He served 9 years as a scout and when the unit was disbanded in 1914 he rejoined the 10th Cavalry and served honorably in the World War. This photo was taken when Jefferson was in the 10th Cavalry. The site is at the front of the fort, Las Moras Creek is behind the tree. (Courtesy of William "Dub" Warrior)

SEMINOLE-NEGRO INDIAN SCOUT DETACHMENT ON PARADE, C. 1910. Sixteen mounted scouts on parade in front of Quarters No. 6–7. Although no longer of any practical use to the Army, the detachment continued to serve into the new century. Fathers and sons served side-by-side, each new generation becoming scouts. Soldiering and scouting came naturally to these men whose quiet pride, dependable performance, and habitual courage made them perhaps the most distinguished auxiliary unit in U.S. Army history. (U.S. Army Military History Institute)

SEMINOLE-NEGRO INDIAN SCOUT DETACHMENT COLOR GUARD, C. 1910. This photo was taken at the same review as the photo above. The color guard has moved forward and is presenting the detachment's colors to the reviewing officer, scout Fay July, on the left. The detachment guidon snapping in the breeze is scarlet for Indian scouts; however, the white lettering and crossed arrows insignia are non-standard. (U.S. Army Military History Institute)

SEMINOLE SPRING, SEMINOLE CANYON STATE HISTORICAL PARK. One of the enduring legacies of the scouts is the place names now associated with their deeds. Emmitt "Pancho" Brotherton, manager of Seminole Canyon State Historical Park, waters his horse Rio from the spring on the floor of Seminole Canyon in front of the natural rock shelter where the scouts habitually camped on their campaigns into the Lower Pecos. (Photo by the author)

MEYERS SPRING, TERRELL COUNTY, TEXAS. Meyers Spring was an U.S. Army outpost, secured by soldiers from Fort Clark. The presence of soldiers in the Trans-Pecos following the Civil War served first to deal with Indian depredations, providing security for travelers on the Lower Road, and then to secure the route of the Southern Pacific Railroad and crossings on the Pecos River. It was Bullis and his scouts who first established a road into and out of the Pecos canyon, making a wagon crossing practical and opening the country west of the Pecos. Bullis at one time owned Meyers Spring. The scouts spent countless days and nights here. Twenty years after relinquishing command of the scouts, Major Bullis returned to Meyers Spring in 1901 and erected the limestone tank at the bottom of the photo. The cliff face has one of the finest rock art panels in North America. (Photo by the author)

The Last Of The Seminole Negro Indian Scouts

LAST OF THE SEMINOLE-NEGRO INDIAN SCOUTS, C. 1914. Pictured from left are Carolina Warrior, Antonio Sanchez, Billy July, Isaac Wilson, Billy Wilson, Ignacio Perryman, Jerry Daniels, John Shields, John Daniels, Fay July, John Jefferson, Charles July, and Curly Jefferson, the last surviving scout who died in 1959. (Courtesy of William "Dub" Warrior)

MEDAL OF HONOR GRAVES, SEMINOLE INDIAN SCOUT CEMETERY. To the south and west of the Seminole camp is the burial ground of the scouts and their descendants. Four recipients of the Congressional Medal of Honor are interred here. Since this photo was taken in 1987, the Black Seminole Indian Scout Association, the Medal of Honor Society, and the Boy Scouts of America have all worked to return a solemn dignity to this place. Under the lone twisted oak at the back of the cemetery are the two first sergeants, John Shields and Ben July; the other scouts are in uneven rows out in the hot Texas sun. On Memorial Day a small American flag is placed in front of each government headstone, a garden of flags for the scouts in their final camp. (Photo by the author)

Five

THE QUIET TIME
1900–1940,
THE 5TH CAVALRY

FRONT GATE TO FORT CLARK, C. 1930S. This view of the main entrance to the fort was made into a popular colorized postcard. U.S. Highway 90 is in the foreground, San Antonio to the left, and Del Rio to the right. The commissary building dominates the skyline and smoke rises from the stack at the post laundry. The buildings at left and center are now gone. The tent area on the extreme right is now the site of the Empty Saddle monument. This is the Fort Clark of the 5th U.S. Cavalry Regiment. (Warren Studio, Del Rio)

MAIN POST PANORAMA, C. 1903. This early panoramic photograph taken from the cupola atop the post hospital is often mistakenly identified as a 1890s view. However, the presence of the steel water tower clearly dates the picture to the early 20th century. The Chinaberry trees are gone but the picket fences remain along staff row and "the line." The tennis court

BASEBALL GAME, C. 1905. William Paulding of the 10th Infantry, in his memoirs of service at Fort Clark, observed of the soldiers, *"Their amusements were only baseball and hunting, so that at night they visited the town of Brackettville which was full of rum holes and gambling dens and crude women..."* Baseball was then truly the national pastime and was probably the first team sport

and bandstand are easily identified and soldiers can be seen on the parade ground. The reader should enjoy comparing this view with others in the book and following the fort's march through time. (Collection of Chris A. Hale)

played between posts in the Army. The player in the center of the picture is the third baseman, "who's on first," and the umpire stands behind the pitcher. The field in this photo is behind staff row and next to the hospital (in the photo above, out of view to the left) about where the Youth Center is today. (Fort Clark Historical Society)

TROOP K, 1ST U.S. CAVALRY, FORT CLARK TEXAS, DECEMBER 10, 1903. The soldiers had this superb banquet-size photograph taken as a gift to their commander, for the back is inscribed, "Presented to Captain John D. L. Hartman, by the members of Troop K, 1st Cavalry." The first sergeant is front and center. (Collection of Chris A. Hale)

HUGH S. JOHNSON. Graduating from West Point in the Class of 1903 (he was a classmate of Douglas MacArthur), Johnson was assigned to the 1st Cavalry Regiment, which in 1903 was garrisoned at Fort Clark. His first military assignment made an indelible impression on his memory. *"Full of anticipation, I went to join my regiment at Fort Clark, Texas, 12 miles from the railroad and 25 miles north of Del Rio on the Rio Grande. It was an antebellum post, put there to guard the marches from the Comanche's. I lived in one of the oldest adobe houses, built 80 years ago. Indeed there were only a few modern quarters there, no conveniences, and the slenderest communication with the outside world. But as I look back, it was a young man's paradise and I had more fun in the years I was stationed there and at San Antonio than in any of my life. Built on a slight rise from a mesquite covered limestone plain of illimitable extent, it guarded one of the finest and largest never-failing well-springs in the country, Las Moras River flowing through some underground limestone channel into the open. The mesquite was full of quail. The Pinto was full of fish. Ducks came in season to near-by lakes. You didn't have to go far for bear, deer, or javelina. There was no prohibition and the 1st Cavalry Mess and Club was one of the best provided in the Army. You could buy a polo pony for $5 and among all the 15 regiments of cavalry, there was none*

74

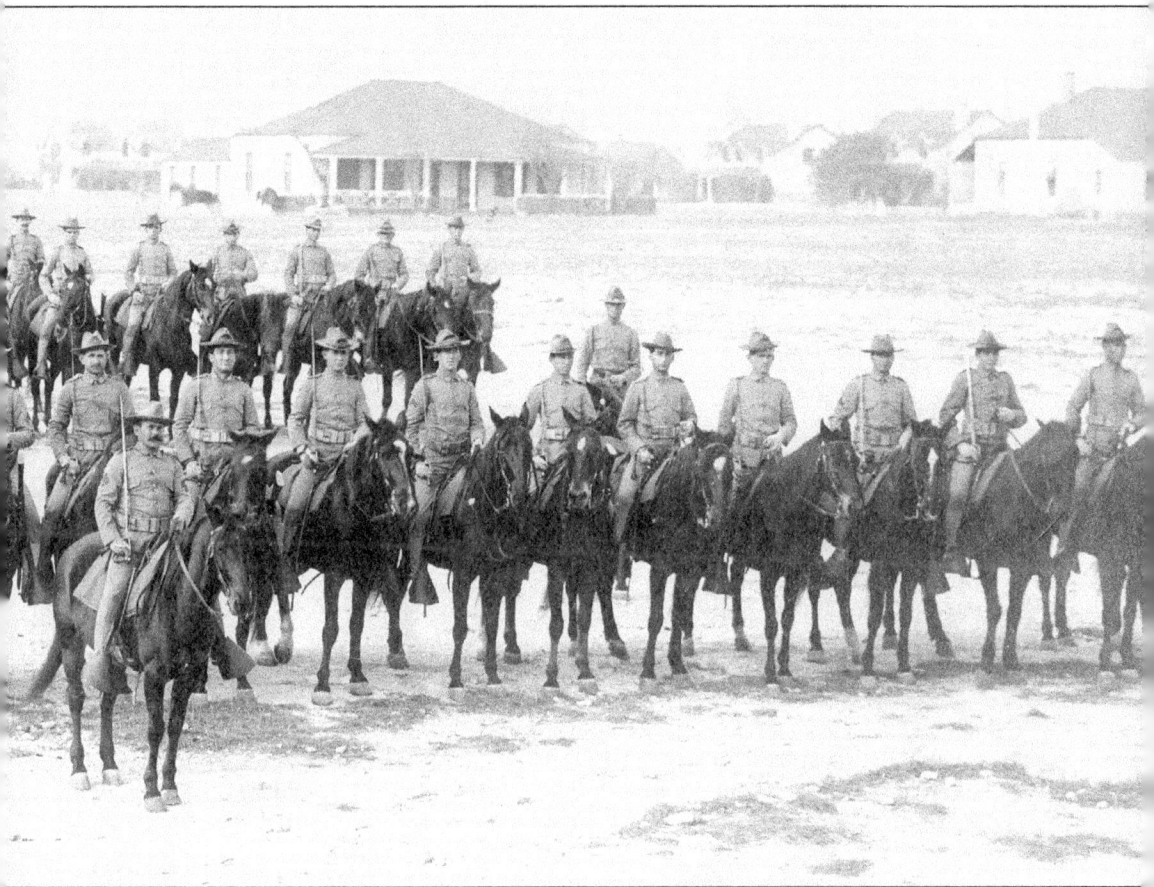

like the 1st. As I have said, the (officer's) club was above reproach and there was all outdoors and over 800 horses to absorb anybody's youthful ebullience. Across the creek was a typical frontier town rejoicing in soldier saloons with such names as 'Bucket of Blood' and 'Blue Goose' and everything that goes with them, everything. [A product of F.D.R.'s New Deal was the National Recovery Administration (NRA), which was the greatest social and economic experiment of its time or perhaps our age. To head the NRA as administrator the president named Gen. Hugh S. Johnson and at this job he gained national recognition.] (U.S. Military Academy Archives)

CORPORAL CHARLES MCNAIR, "L" TROOP, 1ST CAVALRY, FORT CLARK, TEXAS, NOVEMBER 25, 1903. (Fort Clark Historical Society)

TROOPER ELY RABINOWITZ, "H" TROOP, 14 CAVALRY, C. 1915. The 14th Cavalry served at Fort Clark, 1912–1916. This soldier is wearing both a Marksman badge and Expert Rifleman badge. (Fort Clark Historical Society)

PAY CALL, C. 1909. Soldiers gather in front of the two-story cavalry barracks to report for pay. Note the casual nature of the "formation." Payday, more frequently than not, meant a night in Brackettville and several days in the guardhouse! The site today is the intersection between Patton and Bullis Halls. (Author's Collection)

13TH CAVALRY PARADE IN MEMORY OF COLONEL ROOSEVELT (THEODORE JR.), FORT CLARK, TEXAS, JANUARY 8, 1919. This image is the right section of a larger panoramic photograph taken by W.W. Murff of San Antonio. It provides an excellent view of a remodeled bandstand, soldiers on the roof of the hospital, mule-drawn escort wagons, and the Commanding Officer's quarters (now the Wainwright House) just two months after Armistice Day. (Courtesy of Dr. James Moore)

SERGEANT CARL EKMARK, BAND 14TH CAVALRY, REGIMENTAL PHOTOGRAPHER, c. 1916. Official soldier photographers were normally products of the U.S. Army Signal Corps. However, innovative commanders often selected a talented soldier from the ranks and made them the "regimental photographer." Carl Ekmark was discharged following the World War and established a successful photography business in San Antonio. The reader should note that Carl Ekmark took the majority of 1930s photos in this chapter. He not only was a professional photographer of considerable talent but also knew soldiers and Fort Clark personally. His images capture the spirit of soldiering in the "quiet time" between the World Wars. (Fort Clark Historical Society)

13TH CAVALRY IN PHYSICAL TRAINING, FORT CLARK, TEXAS, JANUARY 2, 1919. This is the first of several panoramic photographs that must be broken into four sections for publication (the original photograph is five feet long). The 13th Cavalry served at Fort Clark 1917–1921. There are over 400 soldiers in the full image. This section includes the regimental band and considerable repair taking place to the officers' quarters in the background, to include workers on the roof of the quarters on the right. (Fort Clark Historical Society)

13TH CAVALRY IN PHYSICAL TRAINING, FORT CLARK, TEXAS, JANUARY 2, 1919. The instructor is on his platform, campaign hats are in neat rows, and the ever-present dog looks on. The distinct shadows in this photo indicate it is late afternoon. A horse drawn wagon moves slowly down the street behind the formation towards the lone tree on "the line." (Fort Clark Historical Society)

13TH CAVALRY IN PHYSICAL TRAINING, FORT CLARK, TEXAS, JANUARY 2, 1919. The men are spread in a formation that employs "double-arm interval," creating a distance between soldiers that will allow for safe exercise. Officers are in the front rank as evidenced from their boots, riding pants, and several tunics on the ground. Note the quarters on the left with no roof in No. 20. All the roofs appear to be well-worn or recently damaged by a hailstorm. (Fort Clark Historical Society).

13TH CAVALRY IN PHYSICAL TRAINING, FORT CLARK, TEXAS, JANUARY 2, 1919. These soldiers never made it to France for the war to end all wars. The war ended just six weeks before this photo was taken. Note the man working around the chimney on the left set of quarters and the period automobile on the street. Physical training, or PT, is every soldier's shared memory of the army. When the click, click, click of the mechanical tripod of the panoramic camera stopped on the left flank of the formation, the command was, "arms downward ... MOVE!" (Fort Clark Historical Society)

WILLIAM DENNISON FORSYTH, COLONEL, 5TH U.S. CAVALRY, 1921–1924. Colonel Forsyth, son of Maj. Gen. James W. Forsyth (USMA 1856) of Wounded Knee fame, brought the 5th Cavalry to Fort Clark from Camp Marfa in the fall of 1921. The regiment stayed for a generation. The colonel's daughter, Elizabeth Forsyth Scheuber, shared many of her childhood experiences at Fort Clark with the author. The Forsyths lived in Quarters No. 24 (the Patton House) and Elizabeth was picked up for school every morning by an army escort wagon. She also recalled a social call by a notable friend of her father's from the "old Army," General John J. Pershing. (Fort Clark Historical Society)

THE BRACKETT NEWS, C. 1910. This photo provides a closer look at the buildings lining the east side of Ann Street, c. 1910. The *Brackett News* has served as the community's newspaper for many years. The paper's owner at that time, Will Price, is pictured here in the doorway next to the soldier. Price's young son is in the foreground. (Zack Davis Collection)

FIVE POINTS, C. 1920s. The First State Bank is the centerpiece of this view with the new courthouse behind. This Goldbeck photo captures a serene moment in Brackettville soon after the automobile began to replace the horse on the frontier. This intersection was a very different place once the sun went down and the soldiers appeared. (Photography Collection Harry Ransom Humanities Research Center, the University of Texas at Austin)

SPRING STREET, EAST OF ANN STREET, C. 1920s. Two soldiers head for the movie house in this view of buildings along east Spring Street. The buildings on the left edge of the picture were formerly the offices of the Las Moras Stage Co. (see bottom photo on page 38). The Manhattan Restaurant was a very popular eatery in its day. The building with the tree in front survives today; it now Las Moras Realty. (Collection of Chris A. Hale)

GOLDBECK PANORAMIC OF FORT CLARK IN 1925. Eugene O. Goldbeck, the pioneer panoramic photographer of the Southwest, took more panoramic photographs of Fort Clark, her soldiers, and events than any other photographer. Goldbeck came to the fort every two or three years, with each change of commander. He would photograph the post from the water tower, the regiment from his portable tower, and each unit. This view was taken in 1925. Officers' quarters are in the foreground, followed by the bachelor building, quartermaster storehouse, and two-story barracks. Brackettville is in the distance. (Photography Collection Harry Ransom Humanities Research Center, the University of Texas at Austin)

GOLDBECK PANORAMIC OF FORT CLARK IN 1925. In the foreground an officer cleans the windshield of his automobile. A lone oak tree survives in front of Quarters No. 16. Across the parade ground are the enlisted barracks with stables behind, the post hospital, and the bandstand. (Photography Collection Harry Ransom Humanities Research Center, the University of Texas at Austin)

GOLDBECK PANORAMIC OF FORT CLARK IN 1925. The photo, which is 53 inches long, was taken from the steel water tower behind the officers' row of quarters. The post headquarters, expanded in 1919, is next to the flagpole, followed by a row of enlisted barracks, the commissary, and the stables. (Photography Collection Harry Ransom Humanities Research Center, the University of Texas at Austin)

GOLDBECK PANORAMIC OF FORT CLARK IN 1925. A wagon sits behind Quarters No. 20 where repairs are underway. From the left are the commanding officer's quarters, tennis court, and staff officers' quarters at the turn. Temporary wooden barracks are in the distance with the airfield beyond. Compare these photos with the same view in 2001 on pages 125–127. (Photography Collection Harry Ransom Humanities Research Center, the University of Texas at Austin)

POST GUARDHOUSE, C. 1930S. The guardhouse served two functions: to house the soldiers on guard duty and to hold prisoners. The building has a central guard room where the soldiers on guard duty slept and ate, a prison room where soldiers accused of minor offenses were held, a cell block where prisoners with more serious crimes were confined, and an office for the officer and sergeant of the guard. The building was designated a Recorded Texas Historic Landmark in 1962 and is in use as the Fort Clark Historical Society's "Old Guardhouse Museum." (Ekmark Studio Photo, Daughters of the Republic of Texas Library)

POST THEATER, C. 1930S. The post theater was built in 1932 on the site of the hose house of the 19th century. Its design is the classic "movie house" art deco style of the 1930s. The building boasted refrigerated air and seating for over 300 patrons. The 5th Cavalry band played outside each evening to attract soldiers to the show. The building was designated a Recorded Texas Historic Landmark in 1998, and is still in use for stage productions and social events. (Ekmark Studio Photo, Daughters of the Republic of Texas Library)

84

WAGON TRAIN 1ST CAVALRY BRIGADE CROSSING THE PECOS, SEPTEMBER 13, 1923. A caliche road, which became U.S. Highway 90, and an iron bridge 54 feet above the Pecos River were completed in 1923. In this Goldbeck photo, taken from the west side of the Pecos, a train of Army escort wagons passes an automobile on the bridge. The bridge was destroyed on the night of June 28, 1954, by floodwaters. (Photography Collection Harry Ransom Humanities Research Center, the University of Texas at Austin)

1ST CAVALRY BRIGADE CROSSING THE PECOS RIVER MAY 21, 1938. Crossing the Pecos was a right of passage for a cavalryman in this twilight time for the horse in the U.S. Army. In the foreground are Brig. Gen. Kenyon A. Joyce, the brigade commander, and his staff. Behind them the mounted column stretches as far as the eye can see up the west side of the canyon on U.S. Hwy 90. The white trace to the left of the road on the west side is the ancient Indian trail. The site of Bullis's Medal of Honor fight in 1875 is only a few hundred yards away. (Ekmark Studio Photo, Daughters of the Republic of Texas Library)

1ST CAVALRY DIVISION MANEUVERS, 1938. The four cavalry regiments of the 1st Cavalry Division converged on Balmorhea State Park in the spring of 1938 for division maneuvers. The 5th Cavalry road marched 320 miles from Fort Clark to participate. This aerial photo of the encampment by Carl Ekmark captures the largest spring-fed pool in Texas, the tent city of the soldiers, and thousands of horses on the picket lines. (Ekmark Studio Photo, Daughters of the Republic of Texas Library)

PACK TRAIN WATERING AT LANGTRY, TEXAS, 1938. The barren country west of the Pecos is the northern Chihuahuan Desert. The 5th Cavalry column with over 1,000 horses and mules measured its progress in terms of watering stops and the cavalry maxim of, "40 miles a day on beans and hay!" Here the pack train animals at the rear of the column are watered from portable troughs at the S.P.R.R. depot at Langtry. (Ekmark Studio Photo, Daughters of the Republic of Texas Library)

1st Cavalry Division Maneuvers, 1939. In the fall of 1939 the aroma of thousands of horses returned to old Fort Davis (abandoned in 1889) when the regiments of the 1st Cavalry Division encamped adjacent to the post for their annual field maneuvers. It must have been an eerie experience for the troopers to wander through the old barracks and across the parade ground where the Buffalo Soldiers of the Indian Wars had served. The troopers from Fort Clark knew the feeling well. (Ekmark Studio Photo, Daughters of the Republic of Texas Library)

Pack Radio Set In Operation, c. 1939. The war in Europe had begun and the U.S. Army had strapped Marconi's invention to the back of a horse! A cavalry officer with a field message book on his leg gestures to a trooper while other troopers look on and try to get the radio to operate. The horses patiently await their next meal. (Ekmark Studio Photo, Daughters of the Republic of Texas Library)

FUNERAL HORSE, C. 1930S. The death of a cavalryman brings on ceremony and ritual unlike any other branch of the service. The rider-less horse draped in black, boots reversed in the stirrups of the McClellan saddle, 1903 Springfield rifle in its scabbard, the reins held by a comrade in arms. The notation on this personal snapshot reads, "F trooper killed car accident." The horse holder is identified as Corporal Corey, "F" Troop, 5th Cavalry. (Fort Clark Historical Society)

FRONT GATE OF FORT CLARK, WEDNESDAY MORNING, JUNE 8, 1938. The 5th Cavalry Regimental Band prepares to play a farewell salute for Brig. Gen. R.C. Richardson on the occasion of his departure from Fort Clark. Troopers of the 5th Cavalry line the entrance road as the general's motorcade approaches. Brigadier General Richardson had just relinquished command of the 1st Cavalry Brigade. (Ekmark Studio Photo, Daughters of the Republic of Texas Library)

CORNER OF ANN AND SPRING STREETS, C. 1939. Soldiers congregate on the street corner at McCabe's Drug Store (a saloon in earlier days) as they had done for generations; only the uniforms have changed. On the opposite corner is the First State Bank. The County Courthouse is visible in the distance, and the old post office has lost its second story. (Photo by Lippe Studio)

TROOP "F" 5TH CAVALRY, C. 1930. Soldiers lightheartedly congregate in front of their barracks for E.O. Goldbeck, the photographer. A 1928 Inspector General report recommended demolition of this barracks building due to severe deterioration. The barracks was rebuilt in 1932 maintaining the original design and appearance, while using modern materials and a stone façade. (Photography Collection Harry Ransom Humanities Research Center, the University of Texas at Austin)

BLANKET TOSS IN THE ARMY, C. 1930S. His fellow troopers toss a recruit high in the air as a KP (kitchen police) and other soldiers look on. The picture on page 47 shows this same initiation in the 19th century. The soldier would get his turn tossing the blanket when the next recruit arrived. (Ekmark Studio Photo, Daughters of the Republic of Texas Library)

FORT CLARK HORSE SHOW, SEPTEMBER, 1939. Cavalrymen took special pride in their horsemanship as evidenced by this photo and the one opposite. Horse shows brought riders from other posts to Fort Clark to compete for unit awards. Here Sergeant Corey of Machine Gun Troop, 5th Cavalry takes Bolivar somewhat awkwardly over a jump (the same then Corporal Corey in the funeral horse photo page 88). (Ekmark Studio Photo, Daughters of the Republic of Texas Library)

HEADQUARTERS TROOP, 5TH CAVALRY BASKETBALL TEAM 1937, NINE TIMES CHAMPIONS. The first sergeant with his whistle and multiple marksmanship badges poses with his soldier athletes, who proudly display their cache of trophies. Organized athletics and competition between units was an integral part of soldier life between the World Wars. (Photography Collection Harry Ransom Humanities Research Center, the University of Texas at Austin)

MONKEY DRILL SQUAD, 5TH CAVALRY, C. 1939. Sergeant Holmes, with whistle in his mouth, gallops his monkey drill squad past the spectators. Trick riding by soldiers goes back to Roman times. Units were understandably proud of their monkey drill teams and the competition between regiments was fierce. The exercise also proved a welcome diversion for the soldiers. (Ekmark Studio Photo, Daughters of the Republic of Texas Library)

91

QUARTERMASTER CORPS COMMISSARY, C. 1939. Constructed in 1892, the Q.M.C. commissary storehouse remains the largest stone building on Fort Clark (see photo on page 43). Full gallery porches were added in the 1920s and the center third story was utilized as administrative space, housing the post finance office. The building at the end of the street on the right of the picture was then the post tailor shop. (Ekmark Studio Photo, Daughters of the Republic of Texas Library)

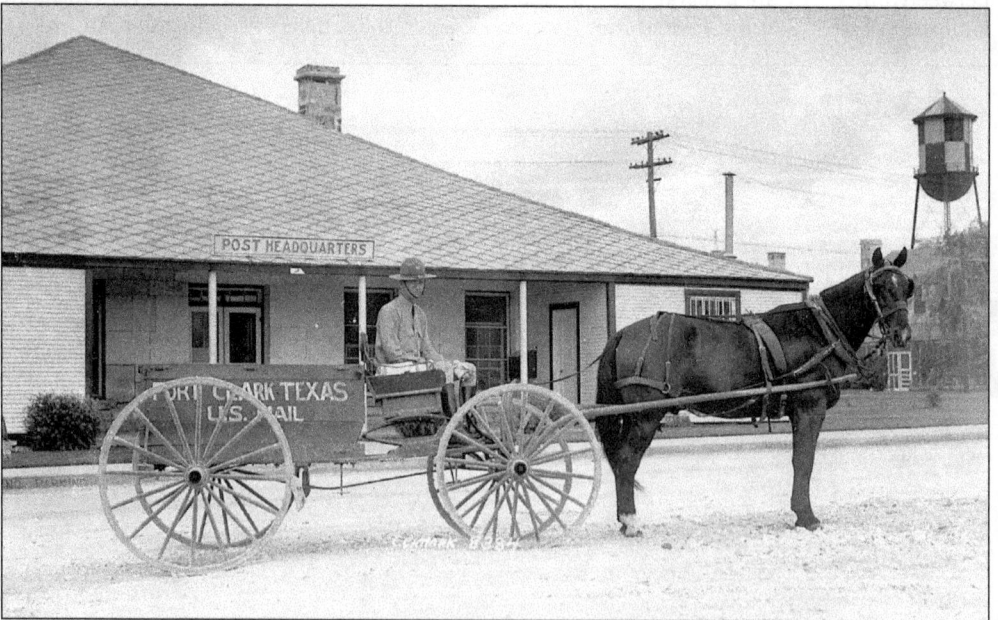

POST HEADQUARTERS AND U.S. MAIL WAGON, C. 1930S. Carl Ekmark had a talent for capturing an ordinary everyday activity and giving it a timeless quality. Here the post mail wagon poses in front of the headquarters building and both driver and horse turn for the camera. The horse and Fort Clark are inseparable, each not complete without the other. (Ekmark Studio Photo, Daughters of the Republic of Texas Library)

NEW CAVALRY BARRACKS, 1932. The lodging for "B" Troop 5th Cavalry improved dramatically in 1932 with the completion of this, then state of the art, facility which included a self-contained mess hall and finished basement with troop offices, supply rooms, and latrines. Built on the site of the 19th-century QM storehouse (see page 43), this building was later the barracks for the Women's Army Corp (WAC) element of the 1855th Service Unit in WWII. Today the building is Seminole Hall. (Warren Studio, Del Rio)

OFFICERS' CLUB 5TH U.S. CAVALRY, C. 1939. The Army does not provide rations for officers. Traditionally, small groups of officers would pool their resources and form a "mess" so that they might eat regularly. This practice evolved into the creation of officer "clubs" where all the officers of a garrison could take their meals and socialize. This building complete with lounge, dining room, visiting officer's quarters, and ballroom was built on the sight of the Quartermaster storehouse of the 1850s. The building is in use today as the Las Moras Restaurant and Lounge. (U.S. Army Signal Corps)

ESCORT TO THE COLORS, 5TH CAVALRY, FORT CLARK, MAY 27, 1939. Saturday, May 27, 1939, would prove to be an extremely long day for the troopers of the 5th Cavalry. These two pictures, taken mid-morning, are of the same event. The formal review began when all troops were assembled (large group in left half of the photo) on the field and Adjutant's Call was

5TH CAVALRY REVIEW, FORT CLARK, MAY 27, 1939. When the escort to the colors was completed, the regimental commander trooped the line, returned to his position, and directed the Adjutant to command, "Pass in Review." Each unit in succession executed a column right from the line and moved towards the post theater, then executed a column left and another column left at the post headquarters. Now on line, they broke into a trot, which carried them

sounded. Here the regimental colors (the flag being dipped, right center), under escort, are presented to the regimental commander and his staff. The buildings, from left, are the post firehouse, hospital, quarters, bandstand, and commanding officer's quarters. (Ekmark Studio Photo, Daughters of the Republic of Texas Library)

down "the line" of officers' quarters for an "*eyes ... RIGHT*" as each unit passed the reviewing officers in the left center of photo. Units left the parade and rode to the airfield for the brigade review (next page). Note the wives and children observing in front of the quarters on the left. (Ekmark Studio Photo, Daughters of the Republic of Texas Library)

1ST CAVALRY BRIGADE REVIEW, FORT CLARK, SATURDAY, MAY 27, 1939. This formal parade of troops was performed on the airfield. A mounted review was surely a spectacle to behold, making every little boy want to join the cavalry. To most troopers, anxious for what Saturday night in Brackettville had in store, it held no charm whatsoever. However, returning troopers have often reminisced with a special admiration, the effortless precision performance of their mount, moving in line with the other horses, and never failing to make them feel like cavalrymen of old. (Ekmark Studio Photo, Daughters of the Republic of Texas Library)

GENERAL J.M. WAINWRIGHT JUST BEFORE LEAVING FORT CLARK. Brig. Gen. Jonathan M. Wainwright (in civilian clothes) and his wife bid farewell to a fellow officer at quarters No. 23–24 (now the Patton House) on September 2, 1940. Wainwright was relinquishing command of the 1st Cavalry Brigade and being reassigned to the Philippines. Five years later, on September 19, 1945 Wainwright was awarded the Congressional Medal of Honor for his "…intrepid and determined leadership…" during the final stand on beleaguered Corregidor. (Ekmark Studio Photo, Daughters of the Republic of Texas Library)

96

Six

MOBILIZATION AND TAPS

WORLD WAR II, 2ND CAVALRY
DIVISION, AND CLOSURE

MAIN POST OF FORT CLARK, C. 1947. This view looks south and captures what would become the Fort Clark National Register Historic District in 1979. The main gate is at bottom left and then the bridge over Las Moras creek. The quadrangle at upper right is the core of the historic fort with the line of enlisted barracks on the bottom and left side, officer's quarters up the right side and across the top, and across the center the theater, chapel, and headquarters. Although this photo was taken after the sale of the fort to the Texas Railway Equipment Co., this is the World War II-era look of the post. Many of the wooden mobilization buildings have already been removed. (Warren Studio, Del Rio)

112TH CAVALRY REGIMENT ON PARADE, 1941. The 5th Cavalry garrisoned Fort Clark for a generation, the regiment departed for Fort Bliss to join the 1st Cavalry Division in 1940. The 112th Cavalry of the Texas National Guard was mobilized in early 1941, and so yet another cavalry regiment stood on the parade at Fort Clark. The guardsmen joked, "Goodbye dear, I'll be home in a year!" (U.S. Army Signal Corps)

SOLDIER MUSICIANS OF THE 112TH CAVALRY REGIMENTAL BAND, 1941. Cavalry bandsmen pose in front of their barracks, now the member services building. Third from the left is First Sergeant Allen Kreiger, who found Fort Clark and Brackettville very much to his liking. In 1976, as vice chairman, Allen helped form the Fort Clark Historical Society. (Courtesy of Mary Helen Kreiger)

112TH CAVALRY REGIMENTAL BAND, 1941. The Regimental Band of the 112th Cavalry plays their daily concert in front of the post theater. The pouches carry each soldier's music. Not only were these soldiers accomplished musicians, but also skilled horsemen. As Allen Kreiger often told this author, "It's one thing to ride carrying a rifle and a saber and quite another thing to ride and play a tuba!" Military bands brought civilized society to the frontier and are a common thread of enchantment throughout Fort Clark's history. (Courtesy of Mary Helen Kreiger)

112TH CAVALRY REVIEW, 1941. "A" Troop, 112th Cavalry passes in review, executing an "eyes right" with their .45 caliber Colt automatic pistols at "present arms." The regiment trained hard while at Fort Clark and the troopers have fond memories of their experience. In 1942 the regiment departed with its horses for the Pacific Theater. (U.S. Army Signal Corps)

2ND CAVALRY DIVISION TROOPERS ARRIVE AT SPOFFORD, 1943. Recruits stand in formation next to the troop train which has delivered them to Texas, a photographer squats to take a picture, and seasoned NCO cadre from the 9th Cavalry of the "old army" take control. A line of "cattle cars," with ramps down, awaits their human cargo for the dusty nine-mile ride to Fort Clark. "You're in the Army now!" (U.S. Army Signal Corps)

RECRUITS ARRIVE AT FORT CLARK, 1943. Under the watchful eye of a 9th Cavalry Buffalo Soldier drill sergeant, 2nd Cavalry Division recruits unload from the "cattle cars" which have transported them from the railhead at Spofford to Fort Clark. In the early months of 1943 over 10,000 African Americans from induction centers in the big cities of the east came to Fort Clark to become cavalrymen. One lesson learned quickly was there wouldn't be much need for overcoats. (U.S. Army Signal Corps)

2ND CAVALRY DIVISION ACTIVATION CEREMONY, FEBRUARY 25TH, 1943. With band of the 9th U.S. Cavalry Regiment in the foreground, the soldiers of the 2nd Cavalry Division assemble on the parade at the post flagpole to be officially recognized as a divisional organization in the Army's Order of Battle. The bachelor officers' quarters is at left and the officer's club at right. These soldiers received their basic training as well as instruction in Cavalry operations throughout the spring and summer of 1943. (U.S. Army Signal Corps)

2ND CAVALRY DIVISION CANTONMENT, 1943–44. This was home for the troopers of the 2nd Cavalry Division. Hastily built in 1942, these temporary frame and tarpaper buildings surrounded by mesquite and brush had pier foundations and literally baked in the south Texas heat. Main post is on the horizon with the Commissary building visible on the left. The salvage operation in 1946–48 removed any trace of these barracks; only the road network remains today. (U.S. Army Signal Corps)

POST LAUNDRY, 1944. A far cry from the laundresses along the creek on page 48, this enormous facility was built to provide laundry service not only for Fort Clark but also for the Army airfields scattered from Hondo to Del Rio. When a prisoner-of-war camp was located on Fort Clark in 1943, the German Afrika Korps POWs were put to work at this laundry. Scales Road is in the foreground. Today, only the smoke stack still stands. (U.S. Army Signal Corps)

2ND CAVALRY DIVISION CANTONMENT LOOKING SOUTH, 1944. This view looks south from the fire station along the road to Spofford. On the left side of the road is the quartermaster cold storage facility at the terminus of the railroad spur from Spofford and to the right of the road is the POW camp. The mobilization for World War II saw almost 1,500 temporary wooden buildings constructed on Fort Clark. (U.S. Army Signal Corps)

2ND CAVALRY DIVISION STABLES, 1944. To the east of the garrison stood a concrete water tower constructed by the German POWs and stables for 5,000 horses. The 2nd Cavalry Division was the largest mounted formation ever stationed at Fort Clark. In 1943–44 the days for the horse in the Army were numbered and the Cavalry Regiments of the Division were some of the last organizations to turn in their horses, forever. (U.S. Army Signal Corps)

POST MOTOR POOL PREPARED FOR INSPECTION, C. 1944. A spacious and modern motor maintenance facility was built below the commissary in 1939. In this photo a jeep speeds past equipment laid out for inspection, to include the motorcycles of the divisional reconnaissance element. The covered area behind the trailers is the wash rack and the building has bays for vehicle repair and a second floor dormitory where the soldier mechanics lived. (U.S. Army Signal Corps)

103

POST CHAPEL, C. 1944. Fort Clark's first chapel opened for worship in December 1941, the Sunday before Pearl Harbor. For the preceding 89 years there had been no dedicated chapel building and religious services were held wherever space could be found. This building is a standard "mobilization" chapel identical to hundreds of others built at posts all over the U.S. just before and during World War II. In February 1943 two Buffalo Soldiers of "B" Troop, 9th Cavalry married local Seminole girls in a double wedding ceremony in this chapel. Sgt. Will H. Raspberry wed Izola W. Warrior, descended from Medal of Honor recipient John Ward, and Cpl. Frederick Shepard married Almeda Hall, whose grandfathers had both served as Scouts. During the salvage operation in 1948 this building was moved into Brackettville and today continues its spiritual purpose as the First Baptist Church. (U.S. Army Signal Corps)

104

NON-COMMISSIONED OFFICER QUARTERS, C. 1944. Adequate housing for non-commissioned officers was always lacking on Fort Clark. There were so few enlisted quarters; many career enlisted men with families lived in Brackettville. The rapid expansion of the post in the 1940s included construction of 25 sets of small but sturdy block duplexes, creating the first enlisted housing area for the garrison. Now referred to as the "49ers," these buildings still function as comfortable homes. (U.S. Army Signal Corps)

MAIN POST FLAGPOLE, 1944. This view would puzzle most of the old soldiers because it includes the short-lived chapel and the wooden second story on the headquarters, but it is still unmistakably Fort Clark. The buildings from left are the Post Theater, the Post Chapel, Quarters No. 6–7, and the Post Headquarters. (U.S. Army Signal Corps)

105

1855TH SERVICE UNIT, 1943. As Fort Clark swelled to accommodate over 10,000 soldiers, the responsibility for running the garrison, which was now the size of a small city complete with its own dairy farm, was given to the 1855th Service Company. The Post Commander was a lieutenant colonel, while the 2nd Cavalry Division Commander was a major general. The 1855th was made up of soldiers from the service support branches such as quartermaster, signal, medical, and adjutant general. (U.S. Army Signal Corps)

1855TH SERVICE UNIT, WOMEN'S ARMY CORPS COMPANY, 1943. The 9th Cavalry Regimental Band plays as the WAC Company of the 1855th Service Unit passes the reviewing party during the 2nd Cavalry Division activation ceremony. These Black women served their country with distinction while at Fort Clark. The company strength was 3 officers and 182 enlisted women, under the command of 1st Lt. Geneva F. Bland. (U.S. Army Signal Corps)

OFFICERS' QUARTERS, BUILDINGS NO. 27 AND 28, AUGUST 6, 1944. Only two months after D-Day and just three weeks before Fort Clark was scheduled to close, a team of U.S. Army Signal Corps photographers undertook a photographic inventory of the over 1,500 buildings and facilities on Fort Clark for the U.S. Engineers Office in San Antonio. Many of these photos are the only visual record of buildings later demolished by the Texas Railway Equipment Co. during their salvage operation 1946–48. (U.S. Army Signal Corps)

SIGNAL CORPS PHOTOGRAPHER BUCK MASTERS, AUGUST 1944. Part of the team of U.S. Army Signal Corps photographers undertaking the photographic inventory of Fort Clark, this soldier also has the pole climbing skills expected of every signalman. The images captured by such men are timeless, visual, historic treasures. (U.S. Army Signal Corps)

POST HEADQUARTERS AND STAFF, 1944. Officers of the 1855th Service Unit pose for an official photograph in front of the building which served the fort faithfully since it was built in 1857, the date in stone relief over the entry door. The Post Commander, Lt. Col. Loren W. Benton, is seated in the center of the front row. However, the true hero in this photo is standing second from the right, Chief Warrant Officer Jimmie E. Ray. In the early summer of 1944 Warrant Officer Ray, the Post Finance Officer, and Captain Sawicki, the Post Civilian Personnel Officer, were assigned the daunting task of closing Fort Clark. Just as Lt. French had experienced during the abandonment of Fort Concho in 1888, Ray faced a staggering duty. Throughout that long hot summer, convoy after convoy of two-and-a-half ton trucks were loaded with post, camp, and station property to be moved to Fort Sam Houston in San Antonio. The date ordered for closing the fort was August 28, 1944. As the day drew closer the only soldiers left were Jimmie Ray and Captain Sawicki. They agreed to stop playing the daily bugle calls, now on a record player, and considered not even putting up the flag but thought better of it. Fort Clark quietly and unceremoniously slipped into history and out of active service on August 28, 1944, when these last soldiers turned out the lights and departed. Corps of Engineers civilians took over as caretakers until the venerable post was declared surplus and sold for salvage to the Texas Railway Equipment Company in October of 1946. Mr. Ray realized his place in the history of Fort Clark when he spoke to this author of those final days: "We just couldn't get everything done and had been ordered to leave." He almost felt guilty. After his retirement from the Army, CWO Ray spent his winters at Fort Clark each year until his passing. (U.S. Army Signal Corps)

Seven

THE GUEST RANCH
BROWN AND ROOT PERIOD

RANCH HEADQUARTERS, FORT CLARK RANCH, C. 1950S. On October 29, 1946, the U.S. sold Fort Clark to the highest bidder, the Texas Railway Equipment Company (a subsidiary of Brown & Root), for $411,250. The new owner sold the lumber and fixtures from the World War II construction and quickly recovered the purchase price of the fort. Almost 1,500 buildings were demolished for salvage. Annabelle Dahlstrom, wife of the owner of the Texas Railway Equipment Company, was the individual force behind saving over 80 historic buildings from the wrecking ball. Herman Brown, of Brown & Root, loved Fort Clark and in the early 1950s opened the "Fort Clark Guest Ranch" to share his treasure. The noble post headquarters building was brought back to life to serve as the ranch headquarters. John Wayne was using the building during the filming of *The Alamo* when on Thanksgiving Day, November 26, 1959, the building caught fire (the result of a faulty kerosene heater) and burned. Today only the shell remains. (Warren Studio, Del Rio)

ENTRANCE TO FORT CLARK GUEST RANCH, C. 1950S. The main entrance to the fort on U.S. Highway 90 changed little from its military days; the new owners even left the "FORT CLARK" iron shields in place. The Guest Ranch era rescued the fort from the fate of other frontier forts in Texas, which for the most part fell to pieces from neglect. (Warren Studio, Del Rio)

FORT CLARK GUEST RANCH HEADQUARTERS, C. 1960S. When the old post headquarters building burned in 1959, Guest Ranch operations relocated to the former 5th Cavalry Officer's Club. The building was ideally suited for its new purpose and came complete with lounge, dining room, kitchen, guest rooms, and ballroom. The building is still in use as the Las Moras Restaurant and Lounge. (Warren Studio, Del Rio)

FORT CLARK GUEST RANCH LOUNGE, C. 1960S. Style and class complemented the historic setting of the Guest Ranch, which was the standard for guest facilities. It was probably not difficult to imagine yourself a dashing cavalry officer when you entered this room. This lounge is now a dining room of the Las Moras Restaurant. (Warren Studio, Del Rio)

FORT CLARK GUEST RANCH SWIMMING POOL, C. 1960S. The third largest spring fed swimming pool in Texas remained the single most popular recreational facility on the property. Since the beginning of the century the cool waters of Las Moras Spring had filled a pool here and beckoned swimmers. Ranch guests spent countless hours in the shade of the oaks that surround the spring and pool. (Warren Studio, Del Rio)

COLONY ROW, FORT CLARK GUEST RANCH, C. 1960S. Officers' quarters on "the line," built in 1873–74, became short-term rental properties where guests could spend a weekend, a week, or a month. The street was renamed "Colony Row" and each set of quarters was named for a famous officer who once served at Fort Clark. Hand-me-down furnishings from the Driskill Hotel in Austin made for little individuality, but it was still a special treat to stay where army families once called home. In 1979 the quarters were sold to private owners. (Warren Studio, Del Rio)

COTTAGES AT FORT CLARK GUEST RANCH, C. 1960S. This "cottage" and the one to the left are uniquely constructed of vertical posts and horizontal logs and are the first permanent quarters for officers built in 1854. Ranch guests may not have realized they were experiencing the same accommodations as J.E.B. Stuart, John Bell Hood, and James Longstreet when they served at Fort Clark. (Warren Studio, Del Rio)

ARMY SERVICE CLUB A.K.A. COUNTRY CLUB, C. 1960S. In 1939–40 the Army built a service club on the site of the original post guardhouse (see page 23). The facility was yet another failed attempt by the Army to keep the soldiers out of Brackettville. During World War II this frame building was an NCO Club. When the fort closed, the Brackettville community used the building as a "country club." Today the Fort Clark Springs Association maintains the building as a social hall for its membership and guests. (Warren Studio, Del Rio)

FORT CLARK GUEST RANCH STABLES, C. 1950S. This is the only stable to survive post-war demolition and was the former stable of headquarters and headquarters troop, 1st Cavalry Brigade. It is not possible to imagine Fort Clark without the horse, "man's noblest companion" as the cavalry recruiting posters boasted. These ranch guests are off to experience the miles of bridal paths along Las Moras Creek. The stables are still in use by the Fort Clark Horse Club. (Warren Studio, Del Rio)

113

FORT CLARK GUEST RANCH AIRFIELD AND HANGER, C. 1950S. The hanger in this photo was built in 1921 and is possibly the second oldest military hanger in the U.S. (Randolph Air Force Base in San Antonio has the oldest). Corporate aircraft, such as the DC-3 in the foreground, delivered prominent Texans the likes of Lyndon Johnson, John Connally, and Lloyd Bentsen to the retreat of Fort Clark Guest Ranch for a weekend of hunting, politicking, and uncompromising relaxation. (Warren Studio, Del Rio)

FORT CLARK GUEST RANCH, VIEW FROM THE CLUB HOUSE, C. 1950S. This view, taken from the balcony of the Officer's Club, shows the meticulous care Brown & Root gave Fort Clark during the period of their ownership. The only evidence that the U.S. Army is gone is that the Texas flag flies from the main post flagpole. (Warren Studio, Del Rio)

114

Eight

REMEMBERING THE ALAMO

FILMING THE ALAMO AND CREATION OF ALAMO VILLAGE

"THE DUKE." John Wayne breaks from filming his epic *The Alamo* in 1959 to pose with the Davis family children and their cousins. From left to right are Bobby and Carol Davis (cousins), Zack, Paul, Alan Kreiger Jr. (cousin), Lloyd Lee, Diane, Nan, and Helen. (Zack Davis Collection)

THE ALAMO UNDER CONSTRUCTION, 1957. Happy Shahan's dream and personal efforts to bring Hollywood to Texas became a reality in September of 1957 when construction began on the first movie location built in Texas, featuring the only replica of the 1836 Alamo mission in the world. More than 1.25 million adobe bricks were made on site in order to authentically duplicate the village of San Antonio and the Alamo mission of the 1830s. (Alamo Village Archives, www.alamovillage.com)

"LIGHTS...CAMERA...ACTION." Cut and print this image as defining a Hollywood set on location. Astride the cable on the right of the photo Wayne stands, hands on hips, with that

BIRDSEYE VIEW OF THE ALAMO AND THE VILLAGE, C. 1960s. This is the south Texas country John Wayne wanted for his epic film. The adobe mission on the left and the village on the right took almost two years to complete. Wayne risked his personal fortune and his reputation on a project he couldn't convince the studios to take on. It was to be the only film in his career he would produce, direct, and star in. (Alamo Village Archives, www.alamovillage.com)

swagger only he could achieve, directing the action which is about to begin. To learn more, see the movie. (Alamo Village Archives, www.alamovillage.com)

JOHN WAYNE AND HAPPY SHAHAN ON THE SET, 1959. Coonskin cap, buckskin jacket, and the proverbial cigarette—that was John Wayne striking fear in all hearts but one ... Happy Shahan's. Happy, in the center, kept close tabs on all aspects of the "shoot" and won Wayne's respect for being his own man. At right is *San Antonio Express News* photographer Hal Swigitt. (Alamo Village Archives, www.alamovillage.com)

GENERAL QUINONES AND MR. CROCKETT, 1960. Mexican General Quinones visits with Wayne on the set. The general was a popular personality on the border, having been a military man of significant achievement and a world-class polo player. One wonders if there was any mention of Santa Anna or the events that won Texas independence and whether or not the story would make for a good movie. (Alamo Village Archives, www.alamovillage.com)

CAST OF *THE ALAMO,* 1960. Standing before the Alamo mission are John Wayne, Richard Widmark, Laurence Harvey, and a cast too numerous to mention, while the Mexican army is silhouetted on the horizon in this classic photograph by Jim Zintgraff. One month before the movie was completed, the cost was at $12 million, and was the largest budget spent on making a film in the U.S. up to that time. (Alamo Village Archives, www.alamovillage.com)

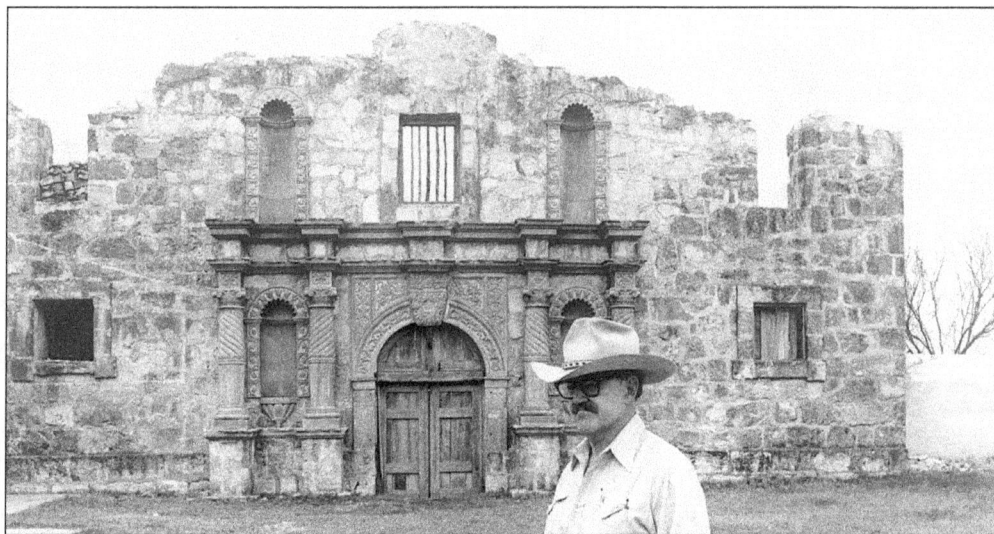

JAMES T. "HAPPY" SHAHAN AND HIS ALAMO. In a land of heroes, Happy Shahan was a hero for the ages! An icon of the Texas film industry, Happy always found time and resources to give to his community, serving as mayor of Brackettville, president of the chamber of commerce, and spearheading civic projects to improve the quality of life. All of these accomplishments were more than enough reason for Gov. George W. Bush and the Texas Legislature to declare April 12, 1995, *"Happy Shahan Day"* in Texas. (Alamo Village Archives, www.alamovillage.com)

119

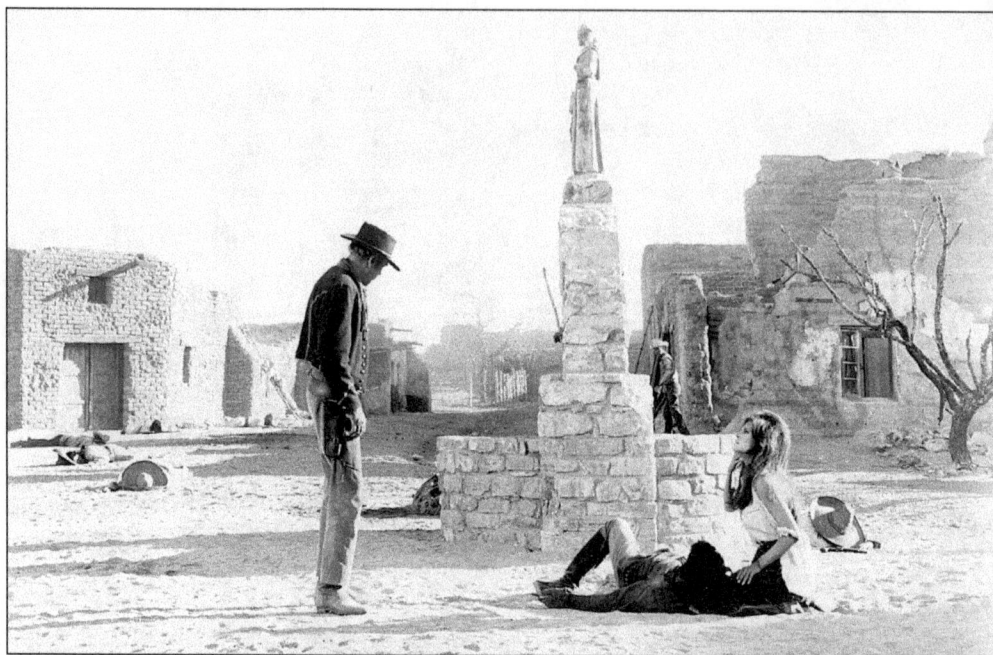

JIMMY STEWART AND RAQUEL WELCH, *BANDOLERO*, 1967. Where movies are made in Texas! Since *The Alamo*, more than 100 major movies, TV shows, documentaries, commercials, and music videos have been filmed here. Alamo Village also serves as a training ground for developing and promoting young talent from across the country, who perform there each summer from Memorial Day to Labor Day. (Alamo Village Archives, www.alamovillage.com)

HAPPY SHAHAN'S ALAMO VILLAGE. This view of the village with Happy riding down the main street was his favorite. For 40-plus years, from Houston in the east and from El Paso in the west, travelers on U.S. Hwy. 90 learned from the distinctive red and yellow billboards that "Alamo Village" was in Brackettville, Texas. Alamo Village is more than a movie set or a tourist destination—it is truly everything that is Texas because two bold visionary men, John Wayne and Happy Shahan, gambled on a dream, and won! (Alamo Village Archives, www. alamovillage.com)

Nine

Legacy of Heroes
Fort Clark Springs and Brackettville Today

"Empty Saddle" Statue, Fort Clark Springs. A cavalry mount stands riderless atop a fieldstone pedestal surround by the guidons of the cavalry regiments that served at Fort Clark. It is a distinctly inspiring monument that leaves a lasting image with the viewer. However, in 1981, when Fort Clark Springs resident Lt. Col. Ralph E. Beard Jr. USAF (Ret) proposed the memorial, he couldn't muster much support for the project. Like so many of Fort Clark's quiet heroes, Beard took the project on himself and a year later, on November 12, 1982, the "Empty Saddle" statue and memorial park were dedicated and have since become symbolic of the fort's proud history. (Photo by the author)

FORT CLARK SPRINGS RIBBON CUTTING CEREMONY, 1972. Nat Mendelsohn, pictured center holding the ribbon, a California real estate developer, purchased Fort Clark in October 1971 for $1 million. Mr. Mendelsohn's showmanship is evident here as local dignitaries and a mariachi band witness the launching of his bold plan to develop a unique combination of country club and private home community he would name Fort Clark Springs. The event took place at the front gate. The commissary is visible in the upper left of the picture. (Fort Clark Springs Association)

BIRDSEYE VIEW OF "DOWNTOWN" BRACKETTVILLE, 1989. Gone are the saloons, mercantile stores, and tailor shops—all gone because the soldiers are gone! Brackettville has never fully recovered from the economic loss of the closure of Fort Clark. In this view Ann Street runs from the left center edge to the bottom right corner. The sturdy limestone buildings built in the 1870s still line its course. The Kinney County Courthouse is in the center right of the picture. Numbers on the buildings refer to the page in the book where a period image can be found. (Kinney County Historical Commission)

122

MEMBER SERVICES, FORT CLARK SPRINGS ASSOCIATION. This building was built in 1931 on the site of an 1874 cavalry barracks (pages 58 and 106) and now serves as the member services facility for the Fort Clark Springs Association. The Association maintains the 1,600 acres remaining of what was once Fort Clark as a membership community with over 700 residents. (James W. Zintgraff)

"THE GREATEST GENERATION." This young infantryman of the 102nd Division stands "on guard" in the rubble of a defeated Germany in 1945 as a conquering hero. When he returned to his hometown after the war, he got a job helping with the demolition of Fort Clark's World War II buildings. He stayed on as an employee of the Guest Ranch and in 1971 continued on with the Fort Clark Springs Association. So for 56 years, longer than any other single person, this gentle unsung hero devoted his life to the service of Fort Clark. Thank you, Juan Avila, for making a difference. (Courtesy of the Avila Family)

PALISADO BUILDING. The only remaining vertical log constructed (cedar post) building in the Fort Clark National Register Historic District. This building was erected in 1869–70, by the Buffalo Soldiers of the 25th Infantry, to serve as a mess room behind their new stone barracks. The later civilian owners of Fort Clark mistakenly identified this building as the *"Robert E. Lee Courthouse."* Regrettably, Robert E. Lee never visited Fort Clark and the building wasn't built until some eight years after Lee left Texas, never to return. The Fort Clark Springs Association completed an extensive restoration and stabilization of the building in 1994. The Fort Clark Historical Society now cares for the building and uses it as a meeting hall. (U.S. Army Signal Corps)

OLD GUARDHOUSE MUSEUM. Designated a Recorded Texas Historic Landmark in 1962, this building now serves as the museum and archives for the Fort Clark Historical Society collections. The Society was formed in 1976 and chartered in 1979, *"... to preserve the history, in fact and artifacts, of Fort Clark, Texas ..."* and since has received, cataloged, archived, and displays over 3,000 documents, photographs, uniforms, and equipment related to that noble mission. (Photo by the author)

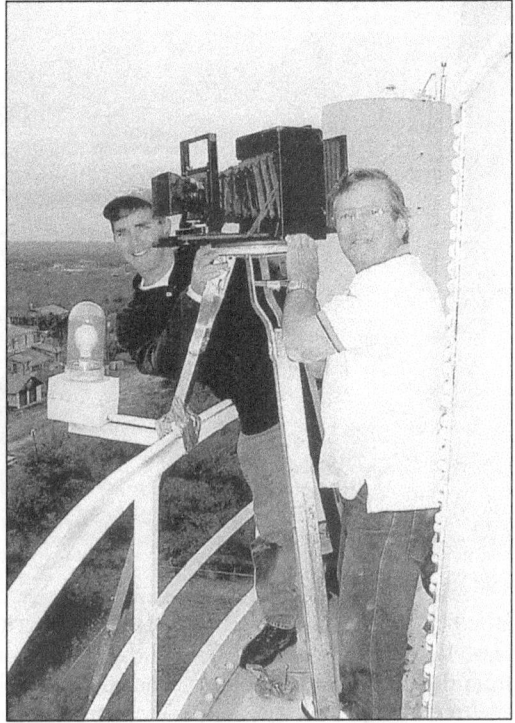

GOLDBECK RETURNS TO FORT CLARK. Photographers Chris Tyler (left) and Ed Goldbeck (right), from the Goldbeck Company in San Antonio, set up their "Folmer Graflex Cirkut" camera atop the Fort Clark M.U.D. water tower on February 26, 2001, to take a color panoramic photograph of the Fort Clark National Register Historic District. Ed's grandfather, Eugene O. Goldbeck, last photographed Fort Clark from the water tower in 1939, using the same camera. (Photo by the author)

BIRDSEYE VIEW OF FORT CLARK, TEXAS—NATIONAL REGISTER HISTORIC DISTRICT, 2001. The Fort Clark Historic District was entered in the National Register of Historic Places in December 1979. The district is the largest under private ownership west of the Mississippi. Certainly the most dramatic changes now from before are the trees and outbuildings. Many of the buildings clearly visible in earlier panoramic photographs are now obscured by the oaks and pecans planted in the 1920s. At upper left is the Officer's Club (Brackettville beyond), then the BOQ, the two-story barracks, and the line of officers' quarters. (Goldbeck Company, San Antonio)

BIRDSEYE VIEW OF FORT CLARK, TEXAS—NATIONAL REGISTER HISTORIC DISTRICT, 2001. In this view the changes to the rear of the officers' quarters are very evident. The garrison flag flies from the main post flagpole and the burned out headquarters building is barely visible through the trees. The middle two multi-story barracks buildings are now motels. The Commissary is on the upper right edge of the picture. (Goldbeck Company, San Antonio)

BIRDSEYE VIEW OF FORT CLARK, TEXAS—NATIONAL REGISTER HISTORIC DISTRICT, 2001. The reconstructed bandstand is on the parade ground, which is now a par-three golf course; beyond is the fire station and post hospital, now the "Adult Center." The commanding officer's quarters, the "Wainwright House," is on the upper right edge of the picture with the pair of tall cedar trees in front. The smoke stack of the laundry is on the horizon. (Goldbeck Company, San Antonio)

BIRDSEYE VIEW OF FORT CLARK, TEXAS—NATIONAL REGISTER HISTORIC DISTRICT, 2001.
Here the Post Theater is on the upper left and then the line of single-story infantry barracks,
now private homes. The concrete water tower pictured on page 103 is centered on the horizon.
In the center foreground is the rear of Quarters No. 14–15 where the photos on pages 32–33
were taken. (Goldbeck Company, San Antonio)

BIRDSEYE VIEW OF FORT CLARK, TEXAS—NATIONAL REGISTER HISTORIC DISTRICT, 2001.
The large two-story building at right center is the "Patton House," named for Gen. George S.
Patton Jr. who served at Fort Clark and occupied Quarters No. 24 while a Colonel commanding
the 5th U.S. Cavalry from July to November 1938. This double set of staff officers' quarters
erected in 1888 was also the Herman Brown residence during the guest ranch era and was
designated a Recorded Texas Historic Landmark in 1990. It is also pictured on page 55.
(Goldbeck Company, San Antonio)

FORT CLARK AND BRACKETTVILLE,
TEXAS ... LAND OF HEROES (Warren
Studio, Del Rio)

The muffled drum's sad roll has
beat the soldier's last tatoo'
No more on life's parade shall
meet that brave and fallen few;
On Fame's eternal camping ground
their silent tents are spread;
But Glory guards with solemn round
the bivouac of the dead.

—Theodore O'Hara 1847

Visit us at
arcadiapublishing.com